EVERY OTHER MONDAY

ALSO BY JOHN KASICH

Stand for Something

Courage Is Contagious

EVERY OTHER MONDAY

Twenty Years of Life,
Lunch, Faith, and Friendship

JOHN KASICH

WITH DANIEL PAISNER

ATRIA BOOKS

NEW YORK   LONDON   TORONTO   SYDNEY

ATRIA BOOKS

A Division of Simon & Schuster, Inc.
1230 Avenue of the Americas
New York, NY 10020

First Atria Books hardcover edition June 2010

ATRIA BOOKS and colophon are trademarks of Simon & Schuster, Inc.

For information about special discounts for bulk purchases,
please contact Simon & Schuster Special Sales at 1-866-506-1949
or business@simonandschuster.com.

The Simon & Schuster Speakers Bureau can bring authors to your
live event. For more information or to book an event contact the
Simon & Schuster Speakers Bureau at 1-866-248-3049 or visit
our website at www.simonspeakers.com.

Designed by Kyoko Watanabe

Manufactured in the United States of America

10 9 8 7 6 5 4

Library of Congress Cataloging-in-Publication Data

Kasich, John.
    Every other Monday: twenty years of life, lunch, faith, and friendship /
John Kasich with Daniel Paisner.
        p.   cm.
    1. Kasich, John.   2. Christian biography.   3. Kasich, John—Religion.
4. Legislators—United States—Religious life.   I. Paisner, Daniel.
II. Title.
    BR1725.K335A3 2010
    277.3'082092—dc22
    [B]   2010006004

ISBN 978-1-4391-4827-3
ISBN 978-1-4391-7218-6 (ebook)

To all who share the journey . . .

"Faith is believing what you do not see. The reward of faith is to see what you believe."

—SAINT AUGUSTINE

Contents

EVERY OTHER MONDAY

ONE

Where Do You Go When the Water Rises?

THERE COMES A TIME IN EVERYONE'S LIFE WHEN THINGS get a little tough, and how we respond to these moments of crisis says a whole lot about our character and our worldview. It says a lot about our faith, too. Personally, I can't imagine facing the storms and dust-ups of this world without a strong sense of a supreme being that takes care of us, watches over us, and creates endless opportunities for us to be the best we can be, even in the face of turmoil and uncertainty. I can't imagine looking ahead at what's to come without the firm foundation of knowing what's come before—and what's awaiting us on the other side.

Now, I'm not suggesting that someone can't make sense of this type of thing without a strong and abiding faith, because a great many people do just that. They look at a mountain or a sunset, and they're transported. They draw comfort in the warm embrace of family or tradition. I can understand that. They find meaning and resonance in the majesty and splendor of the world, and they're uplifted by it. That's great—really!—and yet, for me, the strength to withstand whatever comes my way flows through a sustaining relationship with God and a lifelong, headlong exploration of the Bible. The two go hand in hand, and together they take me where I'm going.

Where do you go when the water rises?

It's a central question, don't you think? How we answer it says a great deal about our faith in ourselves. In one another. In God. And where we look for that answer says a lot, too. I've been thinking about this kind of stuff for many, many years. I think about it, and I talk it through. In fact, some of the people around me recognize that my faith and my search for meaning are such huge aspects of my life that they've been on me to write about them. At first, I stiff-armed the idea. It struck me as preposterous. And presumptuous. I thought, *Who am I to write a book about God and religion?* Me, a guy who'd rather head out to the golf course on Sunday mornings than go to church? Me, a mailman's son from McKees Rocks, Pennsylvania? Oh, I'd written a couple of books, and I enjoyed sharing my thoughts in this way, but a study on faith and the meaning of life seemed a little beyond my pay grade. I didn't think I had it in me to take on such a daunting assignment. Plus, I'm a pretty private guy, and this is intimate, personal territory—and I was never the sort to advertise my faith. True, I'd shared some of my values and beliefs in my previous books, but I'd always stopped short of reflecting on my personal relationship with God—because, after all, it's personal. Nevertheless, a few of my friends kept bringing it up, including some people in publishing who ought to know a thing or two. They kept telling me there was a hunger out there for a kind of ground-level take on spirituality and that I was just the person to give it voice. I didn't know about that, but it was nice to hear.

My friends have an awful lot of confidence in me. That's how it goes with good friends. They push you to believe in yourself, and they fill your head with the idea that anything is possible, and that's what happened here. Slowly at first, but then the idea began to pick up a little steam. Of course, it wasn't just *my* take my friends were after. They knew I'd belonged to a pretty serious Bible study group for the past twenty or so years, made up of some of my oldest and closest friends. They knew we'd been meeting over lunch every other week to discuss issues such as greed and lust and envy and where we go when the water rises, and they thought there might be something in our coming together and our back-and-forth that folks across the country might respond to in a positive way.

At the time, I had no plans to return to public life. I'd logged my time in the State Senate and in Congress, and I was thoroughly enjoying my work in the private sector. I looked ahead to the balance of my "career" and imagined I'd continue working in the media, on the lecture circuit, and in business, and a book such as this seemed to fit right in. Here was a chance to shine light on one value in particular—faith—so I gave the idea some real thought, at around the same time as I started thinking about a return to public life. Suddenly, the idea of a book on faith and a shared search for meaning was appealing to me for the very reasons I'd resisted it at first, because if I went about it the right way, I could take on these big, grand, imposing topics such as God and the scriptures and make them a little more accessible, a little more real. I talked it through with the guys in my study group, and I began to see that I was uniquely positioned to address some of these themes. Check that. *We* were uniquely positioned, because I'd be giving voice to our shared experience.

Look, we're all unique, right? We've all got our own points of view, but in my case, the view came on a bit of a platform, so I was able to put the word out in a way that might be heard. I'd been elected to public office and served the people of Ohio for nine terms as a United States congressman. I'd tried to run for president. I'd hosted a talk show on Fox News and traveled the country giving speeches about what's ailing corporate America and heartland America and how we might set things right. And I'd written those books I just mentioned, which sold enough copies to get me invited back to my desk to write another.

So, as I said, I was intrigued, even as I started to feel the tug and pull of politics yet again. It had been the furthest thing from my mind, until it was front and center all over again. I had been a public servant, after all, and here I was being drawn to a new role on a new stage, where I thought I could do some good.

So there was that, too.

At some point, I decided to take a crack at the book you now hold in your hands, believing that in the small-strokes story of my involvement with these guys in the study there was a much larger story itching to be told—namely, the story of contemporary American men, reaching for real meaning in their lives and in their relationships through discussion and consideration of the Old and New Testaments. Sound a little too high and mighty for you? Well, let me dial it down a notch; let's just call it the story of this one group of American men, me and my Bible guys, looking to make sense of it all in our own way. Like my friends in publishing, the guys in our study push me to reach for more than I might have thought I could handle at first. We push one another. At bottom, we struggle, as I think most men do, to find a place for faith and religion in our lives—only with us, it's not such a struggle, because we go at it together.

There's strength in our numbers. Resonance. Relevance. Resilience. The older we get, the more we've come to understand that the keys to happiness can't be found in praise or money or plaques or whatever it is we seek to accumulate in our workaday lives. Those things are nice, but they're a little beside the point, don't you think? Anyway, that's the mood of the room, among our group. Together, we've helped one another realize that you need to go deeper than trappings or accolades if you seek true happiness and fulfillment and meaning. You need to work at it if you mean to make yourself a better person, or make a difference, or count for something at the end of your days.

Trophies don't make character. Year-end bonuses don't make character. They don't define us. Ultimately, what gives us shape and purpose is the effort we make to live meaningfully and to understand how our time on this earth fits alongside whatever comes next.

Faith, that's what it comes down to. The lessons of the Bible. The insights we draw from one another. In our group, we look to the stories of the Bible as a kind of road map for how to live, how to improve ourselves. It's all right there—the human condition, with all its flaws and in all its glory. But it's not all there in a neat package. No, that would be too easy. You need to peel away all the different layers of implication and context to figure out how to apply those lessons to your own circumstance. As my friend the Rev. Dr. Kevin Maney reminds me, it is impossible to plumb the depths of God. But that doesn't mean you don't try. You need to get at the essence and the meaning, sometimes in a sidelong way. You need to bounce some ideas and interpretations off your friends and see how they look from some other angle. That's what we do in our study.

We're not like any other group I've ever encountered. We're not even like any other group of guys who get together on a regular basis for any reason at all, whether it's to play cards or basketball or to discuss books or business. What we are, really, is a beacon. And a constant. We've been there for one another, in one form or another, for more than twenty years, and I have no doubt we'll be there for one another for the next twenty as well, as long as we're still breathing. We'll keep reading the Bible together until we get it right, and yet even when we fall short, we'll stand as one another's moral compass and spiritual tether, bound by these touchstones.

Let's face it, a lot of us say we're looking for religion and meaning in our lives, but then we go to church on Sunday and cross ourselves and dip our fingers in the holy water and wait for some kind of epiphany. And then we walk out and get into the car and flip on the radio to see how our football team is doing, and we never give God or religion another thought until the next Sunday. That's how it was for me, before our group started to meet. That's how it was for a lot of us, really. And some weeks, that's still how it is, because I'm afraid I don't find God in ritual and worship. He's with me wherever I happen to be. I go to church because that's what you do, but that's not the only point of connection for me. In fact, it's not even first and foremost. I find God in the stories of the Bible, in the random acts of kindness I see every day, in the choices I make and the ways I interact with others.

I find God every other Monday, over lunch with my Bible study guys.

The others in the group are cut in a lot of the same ways. They go to church as they see fit—some more frequently than others. They pray to God as they're moved to do so—some more fervently than others. What we're after, for the most part, is a way to keep God and religion as an integrated part of our lives, and that's one of the hardest things to do. A lot of good, well-meaning people struggle with it. It's not always easy to set aside fifteen or twenty minutes a day of absolute reflection. That's not a lot of time, but you'd be surprised how tough it can be to carve out those moments. We meet every two weeks, to go through these motions in a semistructured way, but I try to do a little bit of it every day. Fifteen minutes—that's the timer I set aside for prayer and reflection, day in and day out. Sometimes I'll fill the time talking out loud to myself. And sometimes I'll talk to God. I can't say for sure that He's listening, although I suspect He is. I've come to realize over the years that it's OK if I take my life's challenges, problems, and celebrations directly to Him. I set it up so it's just as if He's sitting there with me. Some days, it's real work. I'll tell myself I'll do it in the car, but then I can't bring myself to turn off the radio. I want to listen to O.A.R. or the stock report, or maybe I've just gotten the new Pearl Jam CD I want to play, so I bargain. I give fifteen minutes to God and fifteen minutes to Eddie Vedder, because you can't talk to God with Pearl Jam on in the background. You just can't. How would you feel if I was talking to you and I had Pearl Jam blaring on the speakers?

Back to church for a moment. I try to go every Sunday when I'm home in Columbus, but I don't beat myself up if I can't make it. My batting average is a whole lot better than hit-or-miss, but I won't let it hang over my head like a chore. If I can't make it to the early service, I might seek out the late-afternoon service, but it's not any kind of deal breaker if I skip a week or two. I set this out to show that I'm not some fire-and-brimstone holy roller. I'm just a regular guy, going to church, not always paying good attention. Same as most people, right? But as I said, that's not where God lives for me. Anyway, it's not the *only* place He dwells. I see God in all His wondrous creations, and I shout about it in what ways I can, even though it sometimes seems as if most people don't want to hear it. They'll say, "Well, if there is a God, why did He allow this disaster to happen?" Or, "Why does He allow bad things to happen to good people?" That's the classic response of the nonbeliever, and I always answer that it comes down to free will. I say that once God gave us the ability to think and act and choose for ourselves, all kinds of crazy things started happening.

Not too long ago, I was struggling with the notion of how fragile life can be. I took this thought out of bed one morning and gathered my wife, Karen, and our twin daughters and said, "Girls, I love you dearly, but I must tell you something. I cannot control the future. I cannot control life. Only God can control these things, but what I can control is how I worry, so I'm gonna stop worrying about everything. I'll still worry a little bit, but I trust in God to take care of us, to take care of you."

"OK, Daddy," Karen said, pulling the girls in close for a family hug. "We love you, too."

Now, did my daughters, Emma and Reese, have any idea what the heck I was talking about? Probably not, but they knew in a full-on way that I loved them and that I trusted God to help me take care of them, and that was enough. I don't think they gave it another thought. They just moved back to whatever they were doing, and Karen went about her morning, and that was that.

Let's be honest, every parent worries about his or her kids, whether they're nine years old or thirty-nine, and so will I, despite this pronouncement. And yet making a grand state-ment like this in the eyes of the Lord and my wonderful family helps me to dial down that worry a notch or two—because, ultimately, God is in charge.

This was set out for me in no uncertain terms by my former congressional colleague Tom Coburn, who's now the junior senator from Oklahoma. We served in the House of Represen-tatives together, just after my daughters were born, at a time when there was an awful lot of worry in my life. The girls were especially tiny when we took them home from the hospital, each weighing in at about four pounds, and at some point soon after, I had to return to Washington. I hated having to leave Karen and the girls like that, but duty called—and so did I. Every couple of hours, I raced to the bank of phones in the cloak room of the House and called home to see how the babies were doing. They were so fragile, so vulnerable . . . of course, I worried.

I didn't know it at the time, but Tom Coburn was watching me. He stood there, a big, unlit cigar jutting from his mouth, taking note but not saying anything. He's an obstetrician, so he had some experience with nervous fathers, and he finally came up to me one day and said, "Kasich, stop worrying about your kids. They're God's children, not yours."

Talk about a *Wow!* moment, huh? It got me thinking, I'll say that.

It's not just moments of crisis or difficulty that leave us looking for God's hand, because He is with us in moments of triumph as well. Indeed, some people might say that's when He's with us most of all. The Bible is filled with stories of individuals meet-ing with great and sudden success, only to find themselves in dire circumstances because they don't know how to keep humble in the face of it, and when I get together with the guys in the study we seek to understand these dilemmas as well. How is it possible not to return hatred to those who hate you? Or to walk a long, lonely road and become the leader you are meant to be? Here again, faith is key, but we remind one another that it doesn't only come into play in times of extremis. Faith matters when things are going great, too.

That tsunami in Asia not too long ago? You might ask why God created *that*. Indeed, we put the question to the group when we got together just after the story broke, and together we determined that the better, more salient question was why the leaders over there didn't put in a warning system, why they left all those people vulnerable to this type of natural disaster. And then, why did those mud slides occur a couple of years later, when any halfway decent environmental engineer could have told you not to cut down all those trees from the slopes along the coastline? If the government hadn't looked the other way while these people cut down all those trees, because they were poor and desperate for the riches their resources might bring, then perhaps the tsunami and the resulting mud slides wouldn't have been so calamitous. But free will opens up the world to lots of horrible outcomes. And it opens up an answer for why God "allows" these kinds of terrible things to happen—namely, because *we* allow them to happen.

Some folks hear an explanation like that and get to wondering why God doesn't get involved more than He does. Why He doesn't save us from ourselves. It's a good question—the question of the ages, really. In response, I always say, "You might want to ask Him when you get up there." It's a flip answer, I know, but I'm almost convinced that when we do get to heaven, there won't be room in our heads for any of the mundane questions that troubled us on this earth.

You'll note that I say I'm *almost* convinced, because in the end, I can't be certain. I can know a thing in my heart, and in my soul, and in my bones, but then my head gets in the way. I can't help but take a pragmatic view—or maybe it's more scientific than anything else. And yet I still hold fast to the notion of a peaceful, wondrous, unknowable eternity. Yes, I'm *almost* convinced, but that's close enough for right now.

And I've got my Bible guys to help me the rest of the way.

My Bible guys. This is a book about them and their search for meaning as much as it is about me and mine. There are eight of us now, if you count Ted Smith, the Methodist minister we brought in at the very beginning to lead this ragged flock. Over the years, we've counted a few more among our ranks. Some we lost to flagging interest or conflicting schedules. One we lost to proximity—or a sudden lack thereof—although even after moving clear across the country, he still checks in from time to time. One we lost to a sudden death that set our group reeling. And these days, our numbers are sometimes thinned during the winter, when the snowbirds and empty nesters among us retreat to warmer climes—although then, too, folks keep connected by cell phone and e-mail. They want to know what they're missing—but more than that, they want to be heard, even long-distance.

As a group, we look a whole lot different from how we did when we were just starting out, but at our core we're much the same. A little older, maybe. A little thicker around the middle and thinner up top, certainly. A little wiser, we hope. A little more steeped in our beliefs, perhaps. As individuals, we've had our share of struggles and triumphs. We've had some financial or career difficulties. We've had divorce and heartbreak of one stripe or another. We've buried parents and nursed sick spouses and battled our own ailments. We've had our winning streaks, too. We've welcomed children and grandchildren. And on and on. Basically, we've mirrored the human condition, as reflected by eight or ten or twelve men, at various stages in their adult lives, coming together in and around Columbus, Ohio, to find purpose and meaning in those lives by reading the Bible and talking about it and helping one another figure it all out.

From time to time, we'll invite a guest to join us for a session, and our visitors are almost always surprised. I don't know what these people expect, but they come away thinking, *Hey, this is pretty cool*. At least, that's what they tell me afterward. And it is pretty cool. It really, really is. Why? Well, if people are honest about it, they'll all tell you they're searching for some type of meaning in their lives. And here we are, searching. We don't sit in judgment. We're just normal guys, coming together, having lunch, talking about real issues. We don't have our hands up in the air, and you don't see the flames of the Holy Spirit spilling into the restaurant when we open the door. There's none of that. We're just normal guys, regular slobs. It's like that Joan Osborne song where she asks, "What if God was one of us? Just a slob like one of us?"

That's us, just a bunch of slobs, trying to make our way home like the song says, but we have raised our game. We have.

It's become a real marker for each of us. The book. The group. The study. The *routine*. And it's been a highlight on our calendars for as long as any of us care to remember. Lately, we've been meeting at the Monte Carlo, a small Italian joint in a strip mall in Westerville. We've had a few regular haunts over the years, but we're in the middle of a nice run at the Monte.

Nobody bothers us. We're free to ponder and pontificate over whatever passage Ted has assigned for us that week. By this point, we've been through every book of the Bible a couple of times over, and we still don't have a firm handle on it. We have our favorite passages and our long-held views. We have our history and our common ground. We've added a couple of new guys to our group in recent years, to fill in some of the blanks following our losses, and with each new set of eyes and ears, there's a new point of view. Plus, we're all at different stages in our lives, so we see things a little differently each time through.

Every couple of months, there'll be a new server assigned to our table, and I always wonder what runs through these wait-resses' heads as they serve us for the first time. We make an incongruous picture, I'll say that. A table full of men—a doc-tor, a lawyer, a business executive, a financial advisor, a former congressman—coming together in a busy restaurant to talk about things like greed and avarice, ego and envy. Right in the middle of the lunch rush.

We don't really need those Monte menus by this point, but we look at them just the same. Most of us usually order the same thing each time out: soup, chef's salad, heroes, spaghetti. There are specials, but we don't want to hear them, because it's not about the food. This is not a knock on the Monte kitchen—hey, the food's great!—but we're there for the study, and none of us wants to derail the conversation by spending too much time on what to have for lunch. Yet we still have to eat, so there's this odd scene that unfolds, where we can be talking about, say, a passage from the book of Mark. Specifically, we'll get to talking about doubt—one of the grand, recurring themes of the Bible. We'll get right into our thoughts on the assigned reading, after everyone has settled in, which is around the time most wait-resses seem to want to come by to take our orders.

One Monday, reading Mark, we'd started in on our own doubts and fears and uncertainties a beat or two before the Monte waitress had a chance to swoop in and do her thing.

My friend Bob Blair, one of the newest members of our group, was weighing in with his take just as one of the newer waitresses approached him from behind to take his order.

(Not incidentally, there are two Bobs on our current roster, so they go by their last names to avoid confusion. The other Bob—Bob Roach—has been with us since the outset, but he's always been known as Roach, so it works out. Early on, there was also Bob Davies, a well-known Columbus area physician and one of our original members, who died in a plane crash— for some reason, he was always Bob or Dr. Davies. Also early on, there was Bob McQuaid, a guy I met down at the gym, whom we all called Coach. That's four Bobs in all but only two at present. Sound confusing? Well, I guess it is.)

Blair said, "This passage in Mark just blows me away. It stops me every time I read it. There's Jesus, who's supposed to be God. He's up on that cross. He's close to dying, but He's not dying yet. And He says, 'I doubt God.' That tells us even Jesus doubts, so how can we help but doubt?"

Here, I had to disagree. "I'm not so sure that was a doubt, Bob," I said.

Blair: "How can you think that wasn't a doubt?"

Me: "He said, 'God, why hast thou forsaken me?' He didn't say, 'God, I didn't know you were up there.' That's a different issue."

Blair, throwing up his hands: "You're gonna have to explain that one to me."

Here we fell into a number of different sidebar conversations, where we took turns voicing some of the doubts we'd had in our own lives over the years, until Ted tried to move the conversation along and keep our group on point. "Well," he said, "there's a difference between whether or not you believe God exists and whether or not you believe God pays any attention to any one person here on earth. Whether or not it makes any difference. The Greeks believed in a master clockwinder, and some people think that's what started this out, but He didn't have much to do with sinners. So that's a basic issue here."

At around this time, our poor waitress finally muscled her way in, tentatively at first, still not knowing if she should interrupt to take our orders or hang back and let our conversation lose a little steam. The veterans knew just to step up and have at it and that, one by one, we'd break stride and tell her what we'd like for lunch while the rest of us kept right on talking, but this was a tough spot for a rookie. I could see that. As I said, we make an odd picture, talking about this stuff in such a public way, surrounded by local construction workers on their lunch breaks, area high school teachers with a free period, service guys grabbing a bite on their way to or from a call, and anyone else who happens to alight at this pizza and pasta place in a strip mall in Westerville in the middle of a Monday afternoon.

And it's not as if the Monte is such a big, cavernous place that these other people can't hear us. We always sit in the front of the restaurant, right by the window and the open kitchen and the cash register—as if we're in some diorama at a museum. The quarters are close, tight. Folks can certainly hear us, but it's not as if they're hanging on our every word.

We are, though.

Bob Blair gave his order to the waitress and then picked up on Ted's point. "Why would Jesus say that?" he asked. "I mean, He knew He was going to heaven, right? Even with everything that was going on?"

"I'll tell you what," Ted said, in this meticulous, thoughtful way he has of choosing his words carefully. "*You* have somebody driving big old spikes through your wrists and through your ankles and hanging you up on a pole. Then tell me you don't have any doubts."

"But He's Jesus," Blair countered. "He's not like us. If He can't have complete faith, how can we?"

Now it was Bob Roach's turn. "When He was on earth, He was just like you and me," Roach offered. "Felt the same things as you and me. He was manifest, just like you and me. And so, after five or six hours, He was, like, 'Lord, why are you doing this to me?' "

"Yeah, He was just like us," I said, "but without sin. That's the difference maker. He could fend off all this other stuff. Even in the desert, when the devil is saying, 'I'm gonna give you the world, I'm gonna give you riches, I'm gonna give you everything.' Tempting Him. And it says right there in the Bible, He was tempted. It says the devil went away to wait for a better time. So He was man, too, Bob."

"That's a tricky one," offered Tim Bainbridge, our newest member. "Temptation. Not just in the Bible but everywhere you look."

Blair: "How do we know He was tempted?"

Roach: " 'He cried. He wept.' Absolutely, He was tempted."

Me: "Because He was a man, just like us, even though He was God. It's the great mystery."

Roach: "He was just feeling the same kinds of things we all feel."

Tim asked if this might mean that Jesus was tempted by Mary Magdalene.

Ted thought this over for a heartbeat and said, "I'm sure He was. I think that's a very reasonable conclusion, especially if she was some shapely chick wearing a tight outfit."

"Mary Magdalene?" Blair said, somewhat incredulous. "Somehow I don't picture that."

Me, stirring up trouble: "Oh, she was a babe."

Blair: "How do we know that?"

Me: "We know because the Bible tells us so. It says she was a 'prosperous prostitute.' I don't know how you get to be a prosperous prostitute unless you're a babe."

And that's how it goes, essentially. Here the talk happened to be about Jesus and ultimate faith, but more often than not, it's about us. More often than not, it's about how we navigate our days, how we take the lessons we learn from scripture and transpose them onto our lives. We talk through these various issues as they come up in these passages. We talk as men, as friends who have known one another for years and years. We talk as students, wanting to be led. We work our way through the talking points Ted prepares for us before each study. (Or sometimes we don't.) We eat. We ask after one another's families.

We turn the conversation on each other and on ourselves.

Where do *I* go when the water rises? I reach for the Good Book and my good friends in the study. That's the great windfall of our time together after all these years, the deep and lasting friendships that have developed as a kind of by-product. We all knew one another, going in, in a *kinda, sorta* way, but now we *really* know one another. Now we draw from these underlying, sustaining friendships in such a way that it bolsters our shared search for meaning. We've become the first responders in one another's lives, and this right here has been a mighty outgrowth of our group. I've got other friends, from other walks of life, but my Bible guys have become some of my closest friends, because we're working our way through this stuff together.

I suppose we might have come to a similar place on our separate journeys had we thrown in with more traditional study groups in our own churches, but there's something organic about what we've built together. We're not some social-outreach program on a church calendar, which we could attend or not, as we please. Nothing against any of those fine efforts, but here we're accountable to one another. In fact, when you don't show up at the Monte for a session or two, the others will get on you about it. When you don't contribute or offer much of note or insight, they'll get on you for that, too. They get on you, but they know you're *yar*. They know your heart's in the right place. And out of that sense of responsibility and commitment, we've developed fine and enduring friendships. It's quite remarkable, one of the true joys of my life, and it all flows from the unshakable bonds that have been built on the back of our shared search for meaning and purpose.

Together, we can make sense of almost anything—anyway, we'll give it our best shot. We might make a mess of it at first, but we'll keep at it until we reach a kind of consensus or, at least, a place where we can all agree to disagree. I'll listen to their take, and then I'll share mine, and we'll mix and match until we hit on some common ground. In looking back at these ancient texts, we keep one eye focused on the here and now. We invite our eternal perspective to raise our behavior to a higher level.

At the center of a lot of our discussions is the question of how God works. What's He up to? We can go around and around on a subject, but that's what we come back to. When does God intervene? When does He choose not to intervene? Why were there so many people killed in battle in the stories of the Old Testament? Why are so many people killed in battle today? Why are there so many trials we're meant to endure? Does God present us with all these difficulties, or does He merely allow them to happen? These are the kinds of questions we put to one another, and then sometimes we turn it around and make it more personal. How do I forgive somebody who tried to steal my business from me? When do I take risks in life? How do I treat my wife? Are there different places in heaven? What kind of sin is it to lust? How can we steer our children in a more positive, more purposeful direction? When do I stand up and tell people something that they don't want to hear? How much should I tithe?

All the time, people ask me how to get through this or that trial without faith, and I don't have an answer. At this point, my faith is so deeply ingrained that I can't separate myself from it enough to address that kind of theoretical question. But then, these same people might look on at that kind of boundless faith and dismiss it as a crutch, to which I'll always say, "Hey, I don't think a crutch is such a bad thing." We all need to lean on someone or something, right? Might as well lean on the Big Guy. Might as well look to the Good Book for answers and lean on what we find. But there's no magic elixir. When the water rises, the pain is still there. There is no potion or spell to wash away the tears and suffering of this world, but there is a map. There is a place to start, a foundation, and I find it in the books of the Old and New Testaments.

My Bible guys and me, to a man, we'll tell you that when we started this thing twenty years ago, we didn't have a clue. Now we have a clue. Heck, we've got more than a clue. We have a much deeper understanding of life and religion and faith. Along with that, as a kind of bonus, we have a much deeper understanding of one another. You have to realize, we didn't start from scratch on this thing. We all had a core set of values that we brought with us to this enterprise, but that was mostly theoretical. Now we work really, really hard to practice those values. We don't always get them right, but we get close. We're still a bunch of slobs, trying to make our way through this life, but our discipline is greater. Our study is stronger. Our faith is deeper.

We all believe the Bible is inspired. It's the word of God, rendered by man. We don't agree on everything, even as we've come to a kind of shared view. We all get that the stories of the Old and New Testaments are contextual; in other words, you need to understand each chapter in the context of its time. Some of the stories are historical; some are allegorical. On that, most of us are in agreement as well, although we're sometimes split on what's real and what's reimagined. For example, I don't really think it much matters if every animal on the face of the earth was in that ark with Noah. I'll hit this a bit harder, a bit later on in these pages, but for now, I'll just offer that the point of that story about Noah and the ark is that man had gotten so evil that God chose those few He thought were still just and destroyed the rest. Do I believe there really was an ark? Yeah, probably, although it doesn't matter to me how many people or animals were on board. I don't sweat those kinds of details, but we find evidence of the ark and of a great flood in the record, so I weigh in on the side of history on this one. Plus, I've come to believe that the story is much more powerful as truth than as metaphor; it demonstrates that God can ask things of us that seem impossible. I'll bet old Noah looked pretty foolish, building that big boat in the middle of the desert, but that's the whole point. We can all look foolish to others when we answer what we believe is a call from God.

True or not, historically accurate or not, real or imagined, it's never a game changer for me. I don't get too worked up over these distinctions, and I don't propose to have all the answers to life's questions. Just some—and these I've managed to answer in ways that satisfy me. That's the standard I've set for myself, but we've all got our own standards. I'm not so arrogant as to presume that my path to enlightenment and eternity is the only path to enlightenment and eternity. The numbers don't lie. More than half the people on this planet have an entirely different set of beliefs from me and my Bible guys when it comes to this stuff. That's fine. If you ask me how to get to Cleveland, I can tell you the best route that I know. Ask someone else, and he'll give you a whole different set of directions. Go to six or seven others, even, and they'll give you six or seven other routes, and at the end of the day, each one might get you where you're going.

But I'll put it to you plain. I'll let you know why I think my route is the best route. If I think you ought to take Interstate 71 into Cleveland, then that's what I'll tell you. If I believe the way to make it to the Promised Land is to retain Jesus as your lawyer, I'll say that, too. That's the way I've come to look at it. He is our advocate before the Father. He can advocate for anyone—Muslim, Jew, Hindu. But I happen to believe that He's the guy. That's what makes me a Christian. This doesn't mean you have to accept my beliefs any more than I have to accept yours, but this is where I am.

And how I got here is pretty interesting.

TWO

Sing It Like You Mean It

I COME FROM A CHURCHGOING FAMILY.

I grew up attending Mother of Sorrows, my parents' Catholic church in McKees Rocks. At first, I was just like any other kid in the church. I went because my parents went. I went because I was told to do so. I went because that was the routine. But things changed soon enough. I started to pay attention and to participate more and more fully. It began to mean something to me. I noticed the altar boys and thought they had it pretty good. I thought, *Hey, I can do that!* So I became an altar boy at the first opportunity. I was in the fourth grade, and I memorized different Latin phrases, and half the time I had no idea what I was saying, but I said it with great feeling. I learned the rituals and the meanings behind them, and I performed them dutifully.

I was determined to be the best altar boy Mother of Sorrows had ever seen, by a mile. One day, one of the priests took me aside and told me I was doing a great job. He said, "You're the only boy we've got who anticipates what's coming next in the service."

I thought that was just about the highest praise—so much so that I've used the same line in praising others. Or as a point of helpful criticism. It's great advice. It works in any setting. I even tossed it around on the golf course not too long ago, when a kid who was caddying for our group seemed to be one step behind our game. The poor kid was just screwing everything up, so I went up to him after the round and said, "Look, if you want to be a good caddy, you have to anticipate what's coming next." And as I said it, I thought of that priest back home, finding something to like about my efforts as an altar boy.

Fate intervened a few years into my stint as an altar boy. Guy Pirro, commentator extraordinaire at Mother of Sorrows, didn't show up one Sunday. The priest asked me to fill in. I was fifteen years old. I was expected to do readings and to lead the congregation in the service. I can still remember the look on my mother's face as I stepped to the podium—pride, disbelief, and maybe even wonder. (I'm betting that was the look on my face, too!) I guess I did a good and thorough job of it, because I continued in the role every week. The parishioners weren't used to seeing someone so young leading them from the pulpit, and for a brief stretch, I was intimidated by my position, but I grew into it soon enough. I found I had a talent for public speaking—or, at least, an ease with it that allowed it to appear as a talent.

One Sunday, I took myself and my position so seriously that I got a little ahead of myself—and a little egg on my face. I told everyone to turn to the wrong page in the hymnal, and then, when it appeared people weren't singing along with enough conviction, I held up my hands and motioned for the organist to stop playing. Can you imagine? I was barely a teenager, and yet I was taking it upon myself to challenge these folks, many of whom I'd known since I was a toddler. Such brass!

Of course, people weren't singing with enough conviction because I had sent them to the wrong page, so they couldn't help but fumble, but all I knew was that I wanted everyone in church to have the same full-bodied experience that I was having, so I thought it was appropriate to put a pin in the service and offer some guidance.

I stood at the pulpit and said, "Sing it like you mean it."

I hate to admit it, but I actually used those words. Now, looking back, I'm embarrassed at my heavy-handed, overzealous approach, especially since it was my own mistake that had sapped the parishioners of their customary enthusiasm. No one challenged me on it at the time. And yet I'd corrected the parishioners with such conviction that everyone just sang a little louder, as best they could, and when the service was finally (and mercifully) over, an older congregant approached me to tell me ever so gently that I had given out the wrong page.

I was mortified but undaunted. Nothing could shake me from my role, from my rituals. And the fact that these good people had seemed to go out of their way to protect me from my own mortification could only confirm that I was where I was meant to be.

Even as a kid, I had my Bible guys, friends I could talk to about God and religion and all the other stuff you start to think about when you grow up in the church. I can still remember sitting on my lawn one day with my pal Dave Cercone, looking up at the clouds. Back then, Dave wanted to be a politician. I wanted to be a priest. Dave ended up as a federal judge, and here I am running for governor and writing a book about my relationship with God, so you never know how things will turn out. Dave also wanted to be an altar boy, but for some reason, I didn't want him to step into my world. That's how I saw things at the time, as if I had some sort of dibs on the church. I set it up in my head like a proprietary deal. I used to tell Dave he was too fat to be an altar boy, that they didn't have a cassock big enough to fit him. It was cruel but funny. That's how boys are at that age. Dave, for his part, used to call me Pope. Everybody used to call me Pope. Some kid pinned it on me at the playground one day, and it stuck. I spent so much time at church they all thought I'd be pope someday. Even the priests at Mother of Sorrows took to calling me Pope after a while.

Dave and I must have been about thirteen years old, lounging around on these steps we had on our front lawn, and there was a really weird sky that afternoon. It was black and sunny all at the same time. Kind of ominous, kind of beautiful, and pretty much unlike any sky I'd ever seen. Just as we were taking it all in, a flock of birds just burst from a cloud, as if from nowhere. It was the strangest, most wondrous thing.

I turned to Dave and said, "Did you see that?"

He said, "Yeah. Pretty amazing, huh?"

I said, "Do you think that was the Holy Spirit, in those birds?"

Dave thought about this for a couple of beats and allowed that it was possible, and we kicked things around for a while, looking for the hand of God in the weird sky. Neither one of us had any frame of reference for what we'd just seen, so we figured it had to be divine. There was no other way of explaining it.

That's a heavy line of chatter for a couple of thirteen-year-old kids, don't you think? But that was how we looked out at the world, and I think back to that afternoon and realize that even at a young age, I was hungry for talk of God and spirituality. For the most part, despite this one example, I filled this hunger in age-appropriate ways. I didn't really read the Bible as a kid, just the highlights—you know, the Greatest Hits version they give you in church. I said a lot of prayers, but they were garden-variety prayers. I prayed for God to look after my family and friends. I prayed for the Pittsburgh Pirates to win the World Series. The usual stuff. I'd spent all that time soaking up the inner workings of the church, so it came with the territory, but I also remember feeling that all this talk of God was around me, not a part of me. Even as a kid, I could see the distinction. I went through the motions like everyone else. I talked to God like everyone else. But that relationship with God wasn't *inside* me the way it is today. Looking back, I suppose you could say that God was preparing me for this type of relationship, but at the time, I didn't *own* it, to co-opt a phrase from the business world. It was simply in the air and what was expected.

We didn't talk about this kind of stuff at home. We didn't even get close to it. My father was a coal miner's son, and coal miners' sons didn't have a lot of conversations about religion. My father was a man of action, much more than he was a man of reflection. My mother brought up God or religion from time to time but only in an admonishing way. If we kids stepped out of line, our transgressions were somehow judged in relation to our most recent visit to church. My mother would say, "We just left church, and look at you!" As if whatever we were doing wouldn't be so bad if we were caught doing it a little later in the week, after we'd gotten a little farther away from our last visit. As if it made sense for the lessons of the last sermon to rub off after a few days but not right away.

Going to church was just what we did. We didn't have to talk about it or think about it. We just had to go. And once there, we weren't exactly encouraged to talk about our experiences, either. That said, there was a young priest I used to talk to all the time, but he ended up quitting the church and marrying a parishioner, and there wasn't any great weight or spirituality to our conversations. He was a nice guy, and we talked about life and doing the right thing, but he already had one foot out the door of the priesthood, so he couldn't fully respond to some of the thoughts and questions that were bouncing around in my head.

Years later, I finally had a meaningful conversation with the pastor from Mother of Sorrows. This was a man who'd upbraided me when I came home after a semester or two at college and stood while he was holding up the Eucharist, a man who'd known me as Pope for most of my growing up. I went after services to say hello and tell him I was back in town for the summer, and he looked at me and said, "If you ever come to this church again and stand in the back while I hold up the Holy Eucharist, I will knock you to the floor."

He was deadly serious. His reaction took me completely by surprise, because I'd just come from Ohio State, where everything was loose and cool and casual. I was a college man, and I probably thought I was above this type of reproach. Services were conducted in the Newman Center on campus, and everybody stood when the Holy Eucharist was held up, because that's what you do when you're in college. You stand. You take things a little less seriously. You don't pay full attention. I didn't even think about it, and this priest lit into me for being cavalier.

I had it coming, I guess.

He said, "Who do you think you are? In the presence of

God? In all His majesty? Standing there with such irrever-ence?"

There was nothing I could say in my own defense, so I apologized and waited for his anger to subside. Eventually, it did.

The meaningful conversation came a few years after that dressing down, when the same priest was dying of cancer. I was in my late twenties. His name was Father Joseph Farina, and he happened to be in Columbus, so he came to visit me. He was in great pain. I asked him if he was taking any medication to ease his suffering, and he said he was not.

He said, "This is the trial God has placed before me."

His faith made a big impression, because it was the first time I'd seen such conviction on full display. I'd heard about this type of thing. I'd read about it. And here it was, in all its splendor and glory. Here was this man, with a great mind, finding peace and comfort and surety in knowing that his pain was merely a trial he was meant to endure. And knowing full well that he *would* endure it. It opened my eyes, and the scales fell from them. It was shocking. Amazing. And ultimately trans-formative.

Still, that kind of faith was elusive to me then, and it would remain so for the next while. For years, it had been something I'd read about and talked about, and now here it was right in front of me in this once-removed way, so it gave me some-thing to shoot for. Something to think about. And ultimately something to set aside, because, like most young people in this country, I drifted away from religion as a young adult. I'd had it and held it, and then it was gone. I moved away from home, and the tether I'd felt to the church and to all of the meaningful ritual just kind of disappeared. I didn't even see it happening. Then I looked up one day, and there was a huge hole in my life where God and religion had been.

Only I didn't recognize it as a hole just yet.

There was still some of that altar boy left in me, but now I took a knee-jerk approach. If you had asked me at the time, I would have called myself a person of faith, but it was a faith born mostly of superstition and custom. As a young politician, I'd go to church on Election Day and ask God to help me win, because that's what you do. I'd call in the Big Guy at the eleventh hour, like a relief pitcher. And because of the firm foundation I'd had in childhood, I guess I thought I was different from all those other people who practiced this kind of rabbit's-foot faith. I was closer to God than they were, I felt sure. I'd had all that history to draw upon. God was in my back pocket, like a good-luck charm, but He wasn't in my breast pocket, close to my heart.

I'm not in a position to judge other people, but I am in a position to judge the young man I used to be. I could be arrogant back then. I was much more selfish, much more distracted. I had better things to do than go to church or read the Bible or pray to God. Or so I thought. It got to where I didn't even think about God or faith. If I thought about those things at all, I probably just thought, *Hey, I'm OK.* I knew deep down that God was my protector. I knew He would look after me. I had it locked.

It's often been said that when we get to heaven, we'll be surprised at whom we find there *and* whom we don't. I don't know how that works, or even if it's true, but each of us comes at this God and religion thing in our own way. We do our best, or we don't. We get close to it, or we don't. We embrace it, or we don't. Or we turn away. Lately, I've been thinking that the concepts and precepts of organized religion are most attractive to the most people when we concentrate on the do's. There's a perception out there that most religions are built on the don'ts. There's a long list of things you're not supposed to do and all these different temptations you're supposed to avoid if you hope to find some type of salvation. I'm not so sure this is true, but the do's are a whole lot better. They're much more energizing, more uplifting. In any case, these perceptions are often shortsighted, and neglect to consider that the do's and don'ts are only means to an end.

I can't speak for anyone else, but I'd rather be fortified by a positive course of action than terrified by the prospect of a negative one. That's where I choose to place my focus, so that when I see someone who's down on their luck, I try to do something for them. If I'm doing well and I have a little extra money in my pocket, I'll give some away. If someone's moving a little slowly, I try not to breeze past at a hundred miles an hour. I try to slow down and give them a little bit of attention—because, hey, you never know. That person might be an angel in disguise.

Back to me and my churchgoing family. Back to my parents, most of all. They made a real effort on this front. They instilled a strong faith in us kids, a keen sense of right and wrong. Mostly, they helped me to understand that there was something bigger and more meaningful than our lives in McKees Rocks. I took to these notions in a significant way as a kid. It went beyond being an altar boy or a commentator. It went beyond the real sense of belonging I felt when I was at Mother of Sorrows or the way the community cut me slack when I basically scolded everybody for being on the wrong page. I *got* it, I really did. Not in the ways I believe I've *got* it now but in little-kid ways, I guess. So much so that I wanted to be a priest. (Mind you, I also wanted to be president of the United States, so I had a fallback plan in place, even though I can't say for sure which was Plan A and which was Plan B.)

And yet, despite this fine foundation my parents had laid for me, I drifted away from the church as I made my way into the wide world. I suppose this was inevitable, unavoidable. Most of the young people I know go through the same kind of stiff-arming of the practices of their childhood. They look to set off on their own. There are exceptions, of course, but I was no exception. Oh, I made a kind of surface effort to plug back in while I was a student at Ohio State, but as I wrote earlier, things were a little looser on campus than they had been back home. Going to church services there was familiar and comfortable, but it wasn't the same. And I was young enough to think I didn't need the security blanket the church might have offered at that time in my life. I could take it or leave it, I told myself—and for the most part, I was inclined to leave it. It had brought me to this point, no question, but from here on, I would be on my own.

Make no mistake, I continued to believe in God, although in my own way, I came to look on Him as a kind of ace in the hole. I continued to go to church from time to time after college, although it would be a while before I counted myself as part of a real churchgoing community. It was a scattershot effort. I'd go when it was convenient, when somebody asked me to tag along, when there was nothing better to do. I even continued to pray, although the depth and resonance of my prayers were not what they had been or what they would become.

And yet I lived a meaningful, purposeful life, even if I was doing so at arm's length from God and religion. These things were present but not front and center. The values that came along with them managed to stick, so I was happy about that, but when I stopped to think about how I'd drifted from the church, I couldn't come up with any compelling reasons to drift back. The church had been a part of my life, and now it wasn't, and I was OK with what remained from my upbringing, so I looked to whatever might come next with great hope and anticipation.

There was no sadness here, no tinge of regret. I'd been set in my ways as a kid, and as a young adult, I was reset in a whole bunch of new ways, and that's just how it was. My parents had done their part, but the church no longer seemed relevant to me. Not in the ways it had been for my parents. They'd given me a push in the right direction, and after a while I pushed back.

I never expected to hear from my father on this. He was quiet about this type of thing, but my mother was another story. She was the one who'd made religion such a focus in our lives as kids, so I thought surely she'd weigh in and try to set me back on a more purposeful path. And eventually, she did. She tried to talk to me about a real conversion in her life and to pull me into a relationship with the Lord. She was intense about it, but I kept putting her off. I told her I had it all figured out. I listened dutifully and politely but only with one ear. She'd invite me to join her at church when I came home to visit, but whenever I did, it felt to me as if we were just keeping each other company.

I remember a serious mother-son talk about God and religion after I'd gone away to school, when my mother started watching Pat Robertson on television. He really captured her attention, and she told me about him. The conversation stayed with me, as many mother-son conversations do, although at the time, I wasn't impressed enough to tune Pat Robertson in. I paid attention, though. I made a note somewhere in the margins of my awareness. Years later, in one of the great ironies of my life,

I became somewhat friendly with Pat and remembered how my mother had felt a connection to him all those years earlier. Goodness, she was just over the moon about this guy, and now we were in each other's midst. We weren't close friends, but we knew each other well enough for me to reach out to Pat when I thought he was struggling. I'd been out of office for a couple of years, and Pat had been out of the transparently political arena for some time, but he came out with a crazy statement after Israeli Prime Minister Ariel Sharon had been hospitalized with a stroke. He said that Sharon's illness might have been an act of God, a kind of retribution for the prime minister's recent decision to give land to the Palestinians.

Pat Robertson took a lot of heat for these ill-considered remarks, and I felt connected enough to call and offer some advice. I said, "Pat, people think you've made a horrible mistake on this."

He explained that his remarks were taken out of context.

I said, "Pat, out of context or not, you need to do something about this."

Naturally, I wasn't the only one giving Pat advice, and he eventually came out and explained himself and wrote a letter of apology to Sharon. It was the right thing to do, and I'm certain he came to it without any help from me, but the whole time we were talking about this, I kept thinking about my mother, about how she used to watch Pat and tell me what a great influence he was on her life and her faith. Pat and I actually became friendly after this exchange, and I told him about the connection I felt to him through the connection he'd made with my mother.

What were the odds of my mother becoming almost evangelical about this guy and then me turning around all these years later and giving him advice about his image? Of the two of us finding common ground and becoming friends?

Another few words about my parents, John and Anne Kasich. They were children of immigrants, and there was always an outsider-looking-in aspect to their personalities, going back as far as I can remember. My father's family came from Czechoslovakia, my mother's from Yugoslavia. They met just after World War II, when they were both working for the Veterans Administration. My dad delivered mail for twenty-nine years; our house was on his route. My mom eventually worked at the post office, too, sorting mail. They were honest, considerate, diligent, God-fearing people. They had a strong, tireless work ethic. They didn't smoke. They didn't spend a whole lot of money—which worked out just fine, because they didn't make a whole lot of it, either. They had enough, though. They never complained. And they never did without. Their lot in life, their station, became a part of their personalities and helped to form my worldview. In my first campaign speeches, I used to say that my mother would sooner walk a mile than spend a quarter to ride the bus. My father was the same way. And they'd sent me off to school, and eventually to Washington, knowing they'd passed some of those same hardworking, resolute values on to me.

Without meaning to, they offered another push—only this one was cruel and arbitrary and devastating.

They were in their late sixties, in picture-perfect health, looking ahead to a long retirement. They had their pensions and a little bit of money set aside and the comfort of knowing that they'd finally have a chance to put things on pause and relax a little bit. Life was good. It had been good all along, but this was a chance for them to put up their feet and soak it all in.

Lord knows, they'd worked hard enough all their lives. They'd earned a little peace and quiet.

And then, one night in August 1987, they stopped at a Burger King. They almost never went out to eat, but they liked the coffee at Burger King, so they made this occasional exception. It was the best deal in town, they said, because they could get all the refills they wanted.

It was a cool summer night. The roads were dry. There was no reason to think that anything of moment was about to happen as they pulled out of that Burger King parking lot, but a drunk driver came barreling down the road and crashed right into them. I don't think they ever saw him coming.

I was in Washington at the time. It took a couple of hours for the call to get to me, but a doctor at the Pennsylvania hospital where my parents had been taken tracked me down just before midnight and told me my father had been killed and my mother was in critical condition. He spoke plainly, softly, matter-of-factly. That must have been a difficult call for this poor physician to have to make, and it was certainly a tough one for me to receive. In fact, I wasn't sure I'd heard the doctor correctly at first, because your mind starts to do all kinds of strange tricks when you're on the receiving end of such an earth-shattering bulletin. To this day, I'm not quite sure what I said in response or what I did as soon as I hung up the phone. I do know that I eventually made my way to the car and started driving. Actually, the woman I was with at the time did the driving. I was in no condition to drive. I kept hearing the words of the doctor, bouncing around in my head, telling me that my father was dead and that my mother was barely hanging on.

How do you process something like that? How do you cope? How do you even respond and put one foot in front of the other and go about the *business* of responding? Me, without the time or inclination to keep up that good relationship I'd had with God when I was a kid? I'd left myself no course but to flounder.

I was devastated, of course. I loved my parents dearly. They meant the world to me, and it had meant the world that they'd been in such a good, positive place in their lives. They were devoted to each other. For years and years, the church had been a kind of lifeline for me, but recently, my parents had been that lifeline. Knowing that they were still in McKees Rocks, doing their thing, going to church, taking care of each other, is what connected me to the life I had lived as a child in Pennsylvania, to the life I was living now, commuting back and forth to Washington. I found great strength and comfort in knowing that my parents were healthy and happy. And so this piece of news was like a rifle shot that tore right through the picture of my parents I'd carried with me. I couldn't get my head around the idea that my father was gone. The same man who'd taught me the difference between right and wrong, how to catch a baseball, how to stand for something. Everything that was right and good and true about me as a person had to do with everything that had been right and good and true about him. He'd never been much for words or easy sentimentality, but his actions spoke volumes. When you deliver the mail for a living, you put out the very tangible message to your kids that you need to slog through every imaginable ordeal in order to reach your goal. It's right there in the Postal Service motto— "through rain, sleet, and snow"—and it was right there in how my father lived his life. And now a doctor was telling me he'd been killed.

It was too much to think about, and at the same time, I couldn't think of much else. I could think of my mother, of course. She offered her own strong example. She'd set that place for God at our table. She'd taught us what it was to work toward

a goal and to fight for our beliefs. She was still alive when I got
to the hospital, but I never got to talk to her or tell her I loved
her. She died later that morning, and there was that rifle shot
all over again. I suppose I'd known her prognosis wasn't good,
but when you're about to lose everything, you cling desperately
to whatever it is you still have.

At the hospital, I met a young assistant pastor from my parents' new church. They'd moved on from Mother of Sorrows
to an Episcopal church in town, and my mother had been crazy
about this guy. He had come to the hospital as soon as he heard
about the accident, to minister to the family, and I sat with him
for a while. His name was Stu Boehmig. He tried to comfort
me, but I was beyond comforting. He tried to talk to me, but
I was beyond talking to. He tried to tell me he knew just how
I felt, but I couldn't hear it.

I actually lit into him at one point. I said, "How could you
possibly know how I feel?"

As soon as I said it, I regretted it. I had no call to speak to
Stu in such harsh tones. But he understood. He let it slide. He
knew I was grieving, reeling, grasping.

After a while, he said, "John, your mother would be no place
but with her Lord."

Then we sat there for the longest while. Stu could see I
was devastated. He could see I had no place else to turn, and
yet at the same time, I would not turn fully to him. I couldn't.
There wasn't a whole lot he could say that I was prepared to
hear. But to Stu's great credit, he did not give up on me, even as
I appeared to give up on myself. Every day for the next several
days, he sought to counsel me. Every day, he tried to comfort
me. And every day, at least for those first few days, I resisted.
I was too angry at that drunk driver, too busy cursing my parents' tragically bad luck to be pulling out of that parking lot

at precisely the wrong time. I wasn't open to anything but my own grief.

And yet his words left an impression. They kept me standing—not with any great strength or conviction, but at least I was standing. Stu must have sensed that I was lost. And I surely was. I should have known that I had moved away from God. That's what happens when you allow yourself to get caught up in the material swirl of our society, the getting and spending and achieving that tend to define most of our lives. When you're working in Congress, it can be a very isolating, very lonely existence. For some, it becomes a little too easy to look away from the core values that might have called us to public service in the first place. You get swallowed up by all this other stuff—which, of course, is just *stuff*. It doesn't matter how big your office is, or how many points you're ahead in the polls, or what they're saying about you on the Sunday-morning talk shows. But it took Stu pointing it out to me in these gentle terms to get me to realize that I had no place else to turn to get through the days ahead.

Another great irony here was the way my parents died. As a kid, it's what I feared most in life, that my parents would be killed in a car crash. My mother worked in the downtown post office, and her shift would end at about ten or eleven o'clock at night. My father would go and pick her up, and he used to have to drive on a very narrow, very dangerous road. I'd stay at home with my brother and sister and keep a faithful watch on the front door, anxious for the moment when my parents would finally come home. In the back of my head, I kept thinking something would happen to them on that road one night.

I started to think that my parents' accident was a kind of clarion call, the way it brought my childhood fears back into focus. I thought that maybe they were trying to tell me something in death that they'd never quite put into words while they were alive—and they'd sent their Episcopal minister to help turn me around.

Stu's counsel was like a buoy, and now I reached for it. No one could know what I was feeling, but Stu was willing to try to offer some small comfort in those dark days just after my parents' death. He hung in there with me, and at some point, he offered a kind of challenge. He knew my history with the church. He knew I'd drifted away as a young adult. He knew this from conversations he'd had with my mother, and I told him as much when I let my guard down long enough to share a few thoughts. He said, "John, you've got an opportunity here. I don't know where you are vis-à-vis your eternal existence, but your parents' death has opened up a window, and you've got to decide if you want to go through that window. In time, the window will close, but it's open now. Wide open. In time, this pain will ease, and you'll go back to the rest of your life, but while you're here, while it's open, why not peek through and see what's been missing in your life these past several years?"

I thought this was an interesting way to look at my situation. I closed my eyes and heard my own voice, offered from the pulpit when I was a teenage commentator, telling the congregants to put a little more effort into their hymns: "Sing it like you mean it."

Deep down, I knew Stu was right. I had moved away from God in my life, and I had no place else to turn. I thought back to the comfort and safety I used to feel as a kid, enveloped in the embrace of the church and its many rituals. Warmed by God and prayer. By community. By faith and tradition. I realized that these things were missing from my life, at a time when I'd need them most of all. Here, with Stu's unwavering encouragement, I could see that this was indeed a window of opportunity, a chance to reconnect with the faith I used to feel as a kid, with the faith I suddenly realized I wanted to feel once more, perhaps confirming the idea that God permits evil only to the extent that He can redeem it.

Stu said, "That window will close for you, John. It's open now, but it will close. As much pain as you're in now, this will pass. As horrible as things seem to you now, it will pass. Don't blow this opportunity."

It was a real turning point for me, and by the time I returned to Washington a week or so later, I was committed to a journey that would help me determine where I stood with God and my eternal destiny. Where I'd go on that journey or how I'd get there, I had no clear idea, but I knew I'd let God back into my life, through that open window Stu had talked about. Not in a Band-Aid sort of way. Not as a kind of balm or salve to help ease the pain of my parents' death. But as a sustaining, nurturing force in my life.

I'd sing it like I meant it, once more.

THREE

An Open Window

Those conversations with Stu Boehmig in the hospital and in the weeks just following my parents' death were the beginning of an exploration that continues to this day. On a very surface level, they pushed me to seek out opportunities to observe and study once I returned to Washington, but in a deeper, more fundamental way, they helped me to jump-start my faith.

Returning in a full-on way to God and religion is not like turning over the ignition in your car after you've recharged a dead battery. There's no set path to follow, no *How to Put God Back into Your Life* manual to consult. It's a process, and for me, a key in this process was returning to Washington with an open mind and taking the first steps along a path of exploration I would follow for the rest of my life. I wanted to know if this "God thing" was real. It had attached itself to my DNA in childhood, and I'd kind of carried it around with me all these years, without really taking a long, hard, honest look at it. And now I'd reached a place in my life where I needed to know if it was something I could count on, going forward.

Back in D.C., I took up an opportunity that had presented itself sometime earlier. For several years, some of my Washington friends had been trying to get me to attend their weekly Bible study group, and I'd always resisted. The study group was run by a man named Tom Barrett, who worked for the Christian Embassy, an organization dedicated to helping displaced government leaders, diplomats, and military officers seeking purpose and texture in their life and work away from home. As a statement of purpose, that all seemed well and good, but I didn't think this kind of study was for me—and, frankly, it wasn't at the time. Who had time for such introspective pursuits? I wondered. What was the point? I thought this was something I could pursue on my own, if I was so inclined.

Still, I kept hearing from these guys on this, and I kept putting them off. The last thing I wanted was to sit in a chapel with a group of politicians talking about God, because I worried we'd say one thing in there and then go back out and do the exact opposite. If I had been completely honest with myself, I might have realized that I had a wellspring of questions and insights on a variety of spiritual and moral matters just waiting to be tapped and allowed to flow, but I resisted the idea of joining this study group because it didn't seem authentic. It wasn't something I was seeking. I thought I was fine. I just wasn't ready for it, I guess, but when I returned to Washington after my parents' death and tried to cobble my life back together, I started to look on this group as a possible lifeline. I was devastated, shattered, and desperate for any tether.

I was helped along by my great friend John Palafoutas, who

was really the *first* first responder in my life. I use that phrase a lot, to describe my Bible guys and the roles we've taken in one another's lives, the way we answer one another's distress calls before we even put them out. I suppose I could put Stu Boehmig in that top spot, but I hadn't really known Stu when he reached out to me in that Pittsburgh hospital. In contrast, I'd known John Palafoutas for quite a while by this point. I knew he had a keen, inquiring mind and that he had studied to be a minister, although by the time I met him, he had left the ministry. Still, he had a real gift for it, a special flair, and he was an enormous comfort to me during this time. It turned out that John knew Stu Boehmig, a connection I discovered soon after I returned to Washington, and this struck me as the most incredible coincidence. Of course, once I looked at it, I realized it was more logical than incredible. John was from Pittsburgh. Stu was from Pittsburgh. They went to seminary together. It made sense that they knew each other.

Even so, I took it as a sign that everything was connected. John lent me his Bible, and I started to read it. It was a struggle at first. The more I read, the more questions I had—and I wanted my questions answered all at once. I was impatient. I wanted to know everything, fully and wholeheartedly and immediately. Not just in simple, lay terms but in a deep and fundamental way. That open window Stu talked about? I wanted to climb right through it and take in the fresh air of faith and formal religion and be transformed. I wanted to be "blown away," I guess you could say. It took losing my parents to get me to recognize all of this, but now here I was, determined to build a relationship with God, to see if He could stand for me as a source of strength, a point of reference.

I was skeptical, at first, that this kind of pursuit would offer any solace. As I read John's Bible, I found myself wanting a relationship with God, but I knew that relationship had to satisfy me intellectually if it was ever going to make a difference in my life. I wasn't interested in magic or voodoo—no incense, no rote practices, no blind faith. I worked like crazy to figure it all out, and the people who knew me back then must have thought I'd gone nuts. But I was firm in my belief that knowledge is essential to faith. Yes, at some point we are called to walk in faith and trust, but for me it was rooted in *knowing*. I was constantly asking all kinds of basic, fundamental questions, taking nothing as a given, wanting to know if what I was reading was rooted in any kind of authenticity, because for these stories to resonate fully with me, I had to believe with my head *and* my heart, together.

It got to where I was reading as much as I could, as quickly as I could, and then peppering people with as many questions as I could. I finally reached a kind of spiritual fork in the road, where I had to make a decision about whether to keep exploring this stuff, whether it was baloney or real. Or, at least, it appeared to me as a fork. Others might suggest it was a done deal. That God had reclaimed me before I'd even realized it.

Let me touch on that unlikely connection with John Palafoutas again, because I think it's interesting, and it's what drove me back to this D.C. study group in a dedicated way. One of my closest friends on Capitol Hill was Duncan Hunter, a congressman from California. Duncan was one of the participants in the Washington Bible study group, and John was his top aide, so it all tied in. John was like a spirit guide for me in the dark days and weeks after I returned to Washington. I was in deep pain, and John would talk me through it. He made time for me whenever I called and sat with me through some of my lowest moments. That's why I think of him as the *first* first responder in my life, because he'd just drop whatever he was doing if he thought I needed him. That Bible he lent me? He ended up telling me to keep it, and I treasure it to this day. He was godfather to one of my daughters, so he really became an important person in my life out of these dark, despairing moments. And one of the ways he tried to help me was to point me in the direction of Bible study. He said he thought it might do me some good, to sit and talk with a group of like-minded souls about issues and experiences that touched us all.

He encouraged me to attend, and I finally did. As an intellectual exercise, it was fairly fascinating. There were moments when I found the discussion illuminating and others when it was just plain maddening. Tom Barrett did a good job with this group. He was a real intellectual, with great insight, and he remains a very close friend to this day. He spent a lot of time planning each session, trying to come up with creative approaches to familiar topics, and I was amazed at how he managed to get to the nub of every conversation. I recall one session when we were discussing why bad things happened to good people—a key talking point in Bible study, it turns out—when Tom offered an observation that continues to reverberate. He said, "You know, life on earth is like being in a polluted stream. There are a lot of bad things you have to watch out for, a lot of bad people. It all floats on by. Stand in a polluted stream long enough, you can get sick."

It was such a compellingly effective visual, and for the first time, I was able to see the power in discussing faith and religion in straightforward, real-world terms.

The best I can recall, we were all elected officials except for Tom, who, despite his role as leader, conducted himself as just another member of the group. We weren't about to put him on any kind of pedestal, and he wouldn't have stood on one if we did. We met once a week in the chapel of the Capitol. I attended regularly, but I didn't think anything of it if I couldn't make it one week. The other guys were the same way. We came when we could, but our staffs knew to try to keep the hour clear each week. We gave it our best shot.

From time to time, our numbers would swell, such as when there was a scandal brewing in town and elected officials were scrambling for whatever good-luck charms they could stuff into their pockets. During the 1992 banking scandal, for example, when it was revealed that the U.S. House of Representatives had allowed members to overdraw their House checking accounts without penalty, we had thirty or forty members trying to join our group, and I had to laugh, because, of course, you can't just go through the motions of reconnecting with God and expect it to make a whole lot of difference in your life right away. You need to work at it, with a trusting spirit. You need to carve out some time for reflection and study and prayer. You need to rediscover the rites and rituals that were once a part of you and make them a part of you once more.

That said, this renewed pursuit of meaning wasn't about the rites and rituals for me, not in any traditional sense. And yet the culture and practice of religion are the essential underpinnings of our faith. When you're lost in the woods, as I most certainly was, you have to reach for your compass; when you're just going through the motions, you can still manage to move yourself forward, even if it doesn't necessarily get you out of the woods. That's why you've got to take the next step.

I set out these circumstances to illustrate how keenly important it was for me to let religion back into my life. It had played a central role in my childhood, and then I'd drifted away, and now I was back at it, wanting to see if there might be a way to add real meaning to my life. I needed to know if that window of opportunity held any promise for me, not merely to deal with my devastating loss. Now, with perspective and healing, I wonder how people survive that kind of pain without faith. My parents' death began a transformation for me, a journey to discover God and to rediscover myself that continues to this day, as it will continue for all my days. Religion became a source of strength and solace and balance, and in this new beginning I'd made for myself, it was filtered through the common experiences of my fellow congressmen.

With faith, I learned, comes peace. I also learned that it's not an easy road that takes us to God, but with exercise, discipline, and prayer, I make strides. Every day, I make strides. Anyway, I mean to, and this Capitol Hill study group represented a giant step forward for me, toward something meaningful.

Very quickly, I got to where I'd sit with anyone and discuss the Bible, and all of these questions kept bubbling forth in me about faith and purpose and the meaning of life, questions I didn't even know I'd had. I became a real gadfly in our study group, pursuing many different lines of thought and inquiry, but I was desperate to attach some real context and meaning to what I was reading. I'm not so sure the guys in the group knew what to make of me. I'm afraid I became a real thorn in their sides, because in addition to my open heart and my open mind, I also brought my open mouth. I just couldn't keep quiet. I imagine quite a few of them regretted asking me to join, because I took the opportunity to question every single basic tenet of their faith. I challenged everyone, on everything. Reality, that's what I was after. Truth. *Substance.* I asked, "Did Jesus really live?" Or "Why do we think He rose from the dead?" Or "Did He really get crucified?"

I wasn't interested in symbols or dogma, just real evidence

that the search for faith and meaning can have an effect on our day-to-day lives. I wanted to *own* this stuff, not just understand it on an intellectual level. I was determined to get to the heart of what faith really meant. To me.

One of my friends in the study group came up to me after a particularly argumentative session and said, "You ask too many questions."

I said, "There's no such thing as too many questions or too many doubts. Isn't that why we're here?"

I got on a reading kick. I'd long been a big reader, but I'd always reached for histories and biographies. As soon as I started going to Bible study, however, I started reading great thinkers and theologians and philosophers. I steered clear of pop-culture pabulum and focused on the works of Saint Augustine and Saint Patrick, all the way up to more contemporary thinkers such as Billy Graham and Aiden Wilson Tozer—real heavy, dense stuff. Occasionally, I'd make room for a current text, such as Michael Novak's *No One Can See God*, which is a phenomenal book. I go back to it all the time, and each time I take away something new.

When I stepped back and looked at my participation in this study group, as well as all of the reading and reflection I was doing as a kind of complement, I realized how important it all was. I found myself looking forward to each session, but it wasn't enough—just a taste, really. Whatever excitement I'd felt going in, with all of that encouragement from Stu and Tom, it didn't quite take me where I wanted to go. At least, it didn't take me all the way there, because I started to feel that these guys were all careful to say the right thing at all times, which I guess was to be expected in a Bible study group of politicians.

In the best (or worst) example of this, at one of the first sessions I attended, someone stood up and said, "God put me in Congress."

I heard that and thought, *What a presumption, that God anointed you to be a congressman.*

I formed a few strong friendships out of that group, despite myself. And I continued to attend meetings faithfully, despite my feelings that I was falling somewhat short of my goals. And I would have kept at it if something else hadn't come along.

Some months into this exercise, the *something else* presented itself. I didn't exactly see it coming, and I certainly wasn't out there looking for it, but there it was. I was back home in Columbus, drinking beer from a keg with my friend Bob Roach. I hadn't been in the habit of drinking beer from a keg since my Ohio State days, but we were at a Christmas party. There was a lot of noise and merrymaking, and yet we found ourselves talking about matters of weight and significance. Specifically, we started talking about the Bible study group back in Washington. It was on my mind. Bob had been to visit me in D.C. not too long before this Christmas party, and I'd brought him along to one of our meetings, so he knew the players. He understood that I was looking for something more. I told him what I liked about the group and what I didn't.

A couple of beers in, we'd moved on to where I was in my thinking about God and religion. At that point, my head was still a little bit all over the place—and I was still reeling over the loss of my parents, of course—but I told myself that as long as I was thinking about these things at all, I was moving down the right road.

Then it was Bob Roach's turn. He told me where his thinking was. He told me what he was looking for in his life, in terms of God and religion. Some of this stuff had been on his mind, too. I'd known Bob for a long time. He was a successful financial planner and investment advisor. We ran in some of the same circles. I knew he'd been going to Bible study in Columbus for a number of years, which was why I'd invited him to join me in my Capitol Hill group when he happened to be visiting Washington, and I suppose one of the reasons we'd gotten started on this topic was that I wanted to get his take.

What I got instead was a new thought entirely. Bob said, "Why don't we start up a group like that here in Columbus?"

The moment he said it, I knew that's just what we would do. And I thought, *Well, why didn't I think of that?*

I said, "What about the group you're already participating in?"

He said, "I've got time for another."

I said, "Who can we get to lead it?" I'd been to enough of Tom Barrett's study sessions to know that we couldn't patch together a group without a leader at the helm. Otherwise, we'd just be chasing our tails.

Bob said, "I think I've got the perfect guy."

And that's just how it happened. Right there at that keg, sipping beer from plastic cups. It was a nothing-special moment that stands in my rearview mirror as another kind of turning point, and I think it's because our group grew from such humble beginnings that we have kept it simple and straightforward. It's because we were simple and straightforward, too—just a couple of guys looking for insights and resonance and fellowship, thinking we could attract another few guys who might be looking for some of the same things. There would be no bells and whistles, no trappings. We'd just tap the keg and let the conversation flow. That was the idea, and it all started at that Christmas kegger.

Looking back, Bob Roach was a likely repository for my hopes and frustrations on this, and I was a good outlet for his concerns as well. We'd known each other for ten or fifteen years, and he'd always been very honest and direct with me. He was an Ohio farm boy, and he couldn't help but speak the truth in an unvarnished way. He struck me then, as now, as the kind of guy you'd want to have in a foxhole with you. If you're in good with Roach, he'll watch your back. He can lose his patience with me, but that's OK, because he's a man of great character. He fights for what he believes in, and he's not interested in wasting time.

We were a lot alike. His faith was important to him, and he was open to the idea that it could be even more important. He was active in his church but not too active. He believed deeply but not too deeply. And as we stood there at that Christmas party, with our beers in hand, it was clear that we were both looking for something different, something new, something more in our spiritual lives.

A couple of days later, just after New Year's, I went to see Bob at his office downtown. We'd had some momentum on our Columbus-area study group, and neither of us wanted to let it slide now that the holidays had passed. I said, "You really think you can find a minister for us?"

He said, "I think Ted Smith would be great."

I'd never heard of Ted Smith, and Bob explained that he was the minister at his Methodist church in German Village. He said, "Let's hop into your car and go over and see him."

So we did. Ted was in his office; he seemed surprised to see us, but he couldn't have been more welcoming. I liked him immediately. Bob introduced us and told him what we were up to. Ted was intrigued. He struck me as a real straight-shooter type, the kind of minister who wouldn't put up with any disingenuous or halfhearted efforts. Ted remembers that Bob and I were fairly specific about what we were looking for: someone to lead our discussion about the Bible and help us to apply some of its lessons to our time. I liked how Tom Barrett had set things up in Washington, in such a way that he was more like a member of our group than our spiritual leader. I thought we'd do well to borrow that approach here, so I told Ted we didn't want a minister to lead us from on high but to do so from a kind of ground level. And we weren't too sure about this *leading* business, by the way. Sure, we recognized that we needed to be led, but we didn't want to be reminded of it every step of the way. We wanted a leader who would slog through the muck and the mire with us, like one of the troops. Happily, this idea was appealing to Ted, who also remembers that he agreed to take on the job with one proviso: if it turned out after a few sessions that he wasn't the man for the job, we would be candid and tell him so.

Bob remembers that Ted wanted to pray on it before deciding to throw in with us. He said, "Let me think about it." And he did—for two or three weeks. Back then, when we were itching to get started, it felt to me like a ridiculously long time to pray on something as straightforward as whether or not to lead a Bible study, but that was Ted. Bob and I were anxious to get going on this, and we thought Ted was twiddling his thumbs, giving it a good deal of thought. That's another thing I've come to know about Ted: he gives everything a good deal of thought. When he finally came back and said he would lead our group, he insisted on inviting someone else he knew into the group, which was fine with me and Bob, because we hadn't really started reaching out to anyone yet. We needed to fill our ranks, in one way or another, and this was as good a way as any. Ted suggested a doctor named Bob Davies. Like Roach,

Dr. Davies was also one of Ted's parishioners, actually a former parishioner. He'd been a member at Ted's previous church, and the two had developed a close friendship. In any case, we all agreed that Dr. Davies would be a good fit.

My thinking was, *The more, the merrier.* And *Let's get going already.*

With Ted on board, and Dr. Davies as well, we were now halfway to our target number of eight. How we chose that number, no one can say all these years later. It seemed about right. It gave us a bit of a cushion, in case one or two or three of us couldn't make it one week. It spread things out, so that none of us would be able to monopolize the conversation— although, Lord knows, I would certainly try to do just that. And it ensured that we'd have a variety of different opinions and perspectives on whatever matters were under discussion.

To this day, Ted says that he looks back on that ambush visit to his office in January 1988 as a highlight of his ministry. With no disrespect to his congregation or to the fine and inspirational work he does from the pulpit, he considers his leadership of our ragtag Bible study one of the proudest accomplishments of his life. He'd led study groups before, of course, some with long track records that rival our own. And he continues to lead other groups of varying shapes and sizes and staying power. But our group is different, he says, because we came to the pursuit organically. We weren't responding to a flier posted on a church bulletin board or in a newsletter, and we weren't some outreach program Ted was running for his parishioners.

We were a proactive bunch.

Ted says, "It's the difference between preaching to the choir and talking to the guy on the street. At the church, I'm talking to people who are already prejudiced in favor, people who tend to have a genuine and committed respect for the authority and thoughts of the clergy. At the Monte, with this group, there's much more of a give-and-take. They don't take things on faith so much. They're a little more questioning, and they don't look to me as someone who has all the answers. They're definitely not the choir, I'll tell you that."

No, I guess we're not.

FOUR

The Start of Something

WHAT HAPPENED NEXT WAS LIKE A SCENE FROM SOME hackneyed movie script. With Ted Smith in the fold, Roach and I set off to fill the seats at our Bible study group with caring, thoughtful, like-minded souls. We were like George Clooney and Brad Pitt in *Ocean's Eleven*, tapping different people from the nooks and crannies of our lives to help us fulfill our mission. Only here, we weren't looking to knock off some casino. We were looking to use our powers to the good.

(I'll leave it to others to decide whether I was George Clooney or Brad Pitt—although I'm guessing either comparison would be fine with my wife, Karen.)

It wasn't exactly a scattershot effort. Not just any willing participant would do. We were looking for guys with integrity and commitment and passion. Mostly, we were looking for a good, complementary fit all around. The other participants didn't necessarily have to be great friends of ours going in, but we had to know them as people of character. They didn't even have to be deeply religious, in any kind of traditional sense. They just had to be open to whatever we might discover together on this shared journey and willing to shed any preconceived notions they might have had about what Bible study ought to be.

Sound like a tall order? I guess it was, but since we were building this thing from the ground up, we figured we might as well aim high.

The first call I made was to my great friend Ron Hartman. It was a no-brainer, as far as I was concerned. I couldn't think of a guy who embodied our loose set of criteria more fully than Ron, who, even then, was one of my closest friends. These days, I know him as Rondo, although I also call him Red from time to time. I can't say for sure where I came up with either of those nicknames, or even if it was me who came up with them, but they fit. He calls me Jack, but only when he wants to shut me up or put me in my place—two sets of circumstances that seem to come around with more and more frequency the longer we hang around together. It doesn't really matter what we call each other, though, as long as we keep calling each other—and standing in answer.

I can't say for sure why I thought of Rondo on this, either, but he came to mind immediately, probably because I can't think of taking on any new project or endeavor without my buddy Red at my side. He's good company, and I knew that at the very least, he'd get along with whomever else we got to join us, because he gets along with everybody. He's a real guy's guy, as comfortable talking about a ball game as about business or politics—or, I hoped, faith and morality and whatever else we might stumble across in our study. Plus, he's got a great and special knack of fitting himself into virtually any situation.

I'd known Rondo for nearly ten years when Roach and I started putting the group together, going back to when I was a state senator. We met through a mutual friend and hit it off. We spent a lot of time together. We were from different generations, although I don't want to set Rondo off by talking about his age, so let's just say he was an established guy and I was just starting out.

Rondo was a renaissance man, then and still. He reads everything he can get his hands on. He's plugged in to the world around him. He's a lawyer by training, with a strong entrepreneurial streak, but underneath his many and varied interests, there's a warm and generous heart—another special quality I knew we'd need around our table. When my parents were killed, it was Rondo who drove me to Pittsburgh and helped me sort through their estate—another first responder. Recently, he's devoted his professional attention to real estate development, but he's had his hand in a bunch of different deals as long as I've known him. One area he wasn't all that invested in, though, was religion. He'd been raised in a Lutheran church, but, like a lot of us, he drifted away from those moorings in adulthood. We'd never really talked about God or faith or any such thing before Roach and I went looking to jump-start our study, because it hadn't been central to either of our lives. Rondo wasn't affiliated with any church. It wasn't on his radar. But I reached out to him just the same.

"Hey, Rondo," I said. "I'm starting this little group. We're gonna study the Bible. I think you should come."

He didn't even stop to think about it. He just said, "OK."

And that was that. That's Rondo—up for anything. A Bible study group with a bunch of guys he hardly knew was probably the last thing he was interested in at that time in his life, but he was up for it just the same. And I knew he would be, because he's always game. It's what keeps him young. You can call him up any time of the day or night and come up with any crazy idea, and he'll sign on to it, enthusiastically. And here's another great thing: his enthusiasm can't help but rub off. It's infectious, and it's made a deep impression on me over the years. I used to be reluctant to try new things, but after all this time hanging around with Rondo, I'm up for almost anything, too. It's a great way to live your life, don't you think? Instead of saying "Why?" to every unfamiliar prospect that comes your way, you start saying "Why not?" and you open yourself up to a wealth of new experiences.

I've come to believe that Rondo was put in my life by the good Lord to be an encourager, because he's just about the best cheerleader I know. He has a way of making you feel as if you can do just about anything. He's spent a ton of time encouraging me in my assorted pursuits, and I'm profoundly grateful for his support. In fact, he was one of the ones pushing me to write this book, back when I was thinking I wasn't qualified to write about such weighty matters as spirituality and eternity. He said, "Come on, Jack, just give it a try."

He was one of the ones pushing me to enter the race for governor, too, but that's a whole other story.

I like to think I've returned the encouragement. In any case, I've pushed Rondo in the study. I know that full well. He used to tell me he didn't have a whole lot of faith, and that was true when he threw in with us back in 1988. By now, though, he's got more faith than he knows what to do with—and just as much as any of us. He doesn't always recognize it as such, but it's there, in full force. Just to give you an idea, I reached out to him recently to vent and moan about all the different tasks

I had unfolding in front of me. I didn't think I could handle it all, but Rondo set me straight. He said, "Why don't you ask God to help you out?"

It was just a simple conversation, but this was where he went with it—so, clearly, he's grown enormously in his faith. It's gone from being a matter of fact for him to a matter of faith, and that makes all the difference.

Not too long ago, he told me a great story, which I'll share here to show how big a role God and religion now play in Rondo's life. He was out in the field, riding on his tractor, in the middle of a glorious afternoon. (In addition to his many talents and pursuits, he's also a gentleman farmer—and here he was, doing some gentleman farming.) He stopped to take in the scene. The air was crisp and clear, and he was working his own land and feeling pretty great about it, so he allowed himself a brief moment of satisfied reflection. He figured a prayer was in order. He said, "God, I don't deserve all of this." And I guess he surely didn't, because a couple of beats later, he blew out a tire on his tractor.

He told me the story and said, "Tell you what, Jack, I've learned never to say that again."

While I was off recruiting Rondo, Roach was reaching out on Ted's behalf to Bob Davies, one of the most respected physicians in Columbus at the time. This one wasn't such a reach, either, because Dr. Davies was Ted's guy. Ted knew Dr. Davies would respond to something like this, because they'd talked along these lines, so he was a done deal. But Dr. Davies would do far more than just take up a place around our table. Ted knew him to be a very intelligent, very thoughtful man, and he was all of that and a bit more besides. Ted wanted to make sure there was at least one person among us who'd take this thing seriously and make it a priority. Ted knew Roach, of course, but he knew Dr. Davies would help push the conversation in a meaningful way.

From the first time I met him, it was clear Dr. Davies had spent a significant amount of time on these issues. He was inclined toward prayer and reflection. He read the Bible. He went to church with some regularity. That put him ahead of Rondo and me, at least. In many ways, he was more classically suited to this type of study than any of our early "hires," because his thoughts were already turned in this direction, and after Roach went out to meet with him and talk him through what we had in mind for the group, we knew he'd make a good fit.

The thing I noticed immediately about Dr. Davies was how he approached each of the moral dilemmas Ted presented to our group—like a doctor diagnosing a case. He made his own careful assessment of the text, and he listened to each of our separate assessments with equal care before weighing in with his own reconsideration. Nothing was set in stone with him, except for the Good Book itself. From the outset, he was on each of us to interpret every passage as we saw fit, and he was on Ted to make room in the group for every point of view.

One of the most amazing aspects of Dr. Davies's involvement was the fact that he took the time to meet with us at all. It's one thing to express an interest in this type of study but quite another to carve out the time, especially in the middle of a hectic work day. Bob Davies was one of the most respected doctors in Columbus—throughout the state, even. People all over Ohio knew him as a man of depth and passion for medicine and for his great attention to detail. After a while, he took a high-level job with Nationwide Insurance, which pulled him from a lot of the direct patient care he told us he loved but still kept him pretty busy. I was amazed that a guy like that could make time for something like this, but then I realized we were all busy professional people. Heck, I was a United States congressman, spending a chunk of my time in Washington. Rondo was a lawyer and land developer. Roach was a financial planner and insurance salesman. Ted was at the beck and call of his parishioners. We all worked crazy, impossible schedules—and who's to say any one person's time is more valuable or precious than anyone else's?

Still, there's something sacrosanct about a doctor's schedule—probably because we've all been left to wait and wonder about the responsibilities a doctor faces every day. So I was impressed by the mere fact of Dr. Davies's involvement. But my impression didn't end there. One of the ways he stamped our first sessions was with how he sought to understand the stories in a cultural sense. That was his big thing, to consider the lessons and values against the framework of the times, and by our second or third session, he had us all strongly considering his take. The guy was proving to be a real spiritual heavyweight. As a group, we went from having our hard-and-fast views to being completely open to different interpretations, and I have to think Dr. Davies had as much to do with that as anyone.

That put our ranks at five, an unlikely quintet determined to get to the heart of what it meant to live a good, purposeful life, and from there, it took another couple of weeks before we could fill out the group and get started.

At one point in the middle of our recruiting, I got together with Roach to discuss our progress. This was back before the widespread use of cell phones and e-mail, so we weren't in constant touch as we are today. We had to set aside time for this type of thing, so we did—over beers, as I recall, which was only fitting, since our first notion about the study had sprung at a kegger. We compared notes. We talked about some of the people we knew in common who might be willing to join us and about how soon we could get started. To reiterate, our thinking was that we'd need seven or eight guys to make it a viable, workable enterprise. That was our target. With fewer than that, we wouldn't have a cushion against the inevitable travel and scheduling conflicts that might crop up from time to time. With more than that, we'd crowd one another out and lose the sense of intimacy and familiarity we were after.

The plan was to meet over lunch. We all had to eat anyway, so we could multitask. If we set it up for a weekend or a weeknight, it might end up straining some of our family obligations. We were determined to put ourselves in a strong position to succeed with this group, and we knew scheduling would be a big part of that. If the time we set aside didn't work for the biggest possible number, we'd never get any traction on this thing, so we considered every contingency. We were thinking long-term. The "casting" of our group would leave a whole lot to chance and the meshing of our personalities, but the scheduling was something we could control, so we looked to get a handle on it at the outset.

I was bound to Mondays, since I was often in Washington in the middle of the week when Congress was in session. If I needed to get back to Capitol Hill for a late Monday meeting, I could usually head out after an early lunch, so we set aside the noon hour. The other guys had their own constraints as well, but Mondays seemed to work for everyone so far.

It wasn't just Roach and me banging out these details. Once these other guys were in the fold, their voices were just as loud as ours. Everyone agreed that a weekly get-together might be a drag on our work schedules, so we set it up as an every-other-week deal. I was still keeping up with the Washington study group while we were jump-starting our Columbus group, and that was a weekly affair, and it felt to me as if a longer point of pause and reflection would be helpful in this new enterprise.

Every other Monday seemed about right.

We needed a venue, of course. We talked about doing it at one of our houses or maybe even rotating from house to house, but we quickly rejected this idea as impractical. It's not as if we all lived or worked down the street from one another, so we needed a central location. (Dr. Davies didn't even live in town; for most of our time together in the study he piloted his own small plane and planned to fly in for sessions.) We thought briefly about holding the meetings at Ted's church and brown-bagging it on the lunch front, but this setup came with its own complications. Well, I wouldn't exactly call them complications so much as inconveniences—namely, that we'd have to pack our own lunches. Who had time for *that*? Also inconvenient was that none of us was a parishioner, except for Roach, and even though we hadn't filled out our ranks just yet, we didn't want to be bound or beholden to drawing our participants from Ted's congregation. Nothing against Ted's fine flock, but we wanted our group to come together in a more fluid, hand-picked way. After all, as I wrote earlier, if we wanted a garden-variety study group, we could have joined running groups at our own churches.

Roach set off in search of an appropriate setting, while I went looking for a couple more recruits. Happily, the next guy I reached out to wanted in: Dick Vogt, a lobbyist I'd first met in Washington. Dick impressed me as a man of great character. In fact, early on, I had a chance to see his integrity on full display. Before becoming a lobbyist, he'd been an executive at the telephone company, so he tended to push issues in the field of telecommunications. He knew his stuff, but, like all lobbyists, he had his own agenda—and a forceful personality. Early in our friendship, we had a big blowup over some misunderstanding or other. Once we cleared the air, he couldn't have been more accommodating. He said, "John, you'll never have to worry about me misleading you on anything. I might disagree with you, but I'll never mislead you."

And true to his word, he never has. He's one of the most delightful, agreeable guys I've ever met. Forceful, yes, but forthright as well. There's a certain glimmer about Dick that I find enormously appealing. Folks are drawn to him—that's what made him such an effective lobbyist. We'd never really discussed religion or matters of faith, but I thought he'd fit right in, and when I laid out for him what we were up to, he responded to it right away. He even told me about a significant religious experience he'd had as a young man, when a vision appeared to him on a lonely road one Sunday morning, and to this day, he's the only one of our group who's had that type of experience. We all talk to God in our own ways, but Dick's the only one who might have actually heard back from Him, and I think we all envy him the encounter.

The only problem with Dick, really, is that his language can get a little salty. Maybe *problem* is too strong a word here, because it's never really been an issue for any of us, but it is a very noticeable character trait. I've played golf with Dick quite often, and he can't stop cursing out there on the course, especially when things aren't going well in his game. I knew this about him going in, and indeed, I worried that it might be a problem in the study, because it's one thing to run off a string of expletives on the golf course and quite another to start spewing this stuff during Bible study, but as I said, it's never been an issue. He knows when to hold his tongue and when to let loose. He won't clean up his act entirely, but as far as I can tell, he hasn't offended anybody yet, not even Ted.

Next, I looked to my friend Bill Lhota, an executive at Columbus and Southern Power, another diligent, purposeful, intellectually curious person I'd somehow collected along the way. It's amazing how many people you meet during the course of your days who might fit the bill for something like this. At first blush, you might think, *Aw, heck, I don't know anybody who'd be interested in this type of thing.* But then you give it some thought and run through your list of friends and acquaintances and realize that there are a lot of people in your life looking for some of the same things, with the same passion and yearning and curiosity. It just takes talking about it to put it on the table.

Bill and I had met several years earlier through my work in the state legislature and formed a connection. He helped me politically on a number of occasions. He even hosted an event at his home for me, so I had a lot of regard for him. What I liked about Bill for our study group was that he had a curious mind and a genuine warmth. Plus, he already had a deep religious faith. We didn't really talk about God or religion when we got together, because that's not the sort of thing that comes up in a social setting or at a political fund-raiser, but he let it be known that his faith and his church were important to him and his family, and I respected that. I also respected how he spoke his mind. Once, at a dinner I had to attend as a young legislator, he pulled me aside after I'd been holding forth on some issue or other. He said, "John, I've been listening to you talk and talk, but you're really off base about this."

I respected Bill's straight talk at the time, and I found myself thinking back to this exchange when I proposed our percolating Bible study group to him. I thought a guy with the gentle brass to talk so straight with a brash young legislator was just the kind we wanted in our midst, someone who would offer his unvarnished take on these seminal issues as we all reached for shape and meaning in our lives.

With Dick and Bill, we now numbered seven, and we all agreed that was enough to get us started, so we turned to our calendars and came up with a date that worked for all of us. It wouldn't do to launch our study with anything less than full attendance. It had been a couple of months since Roach and I had hatched the idea at that Christmas party, so I was itching to get going. Again, I'd kept up with my Washington study group during that time, because I didn't want to lose the momentum I'd gained on this effort, but I was ready to move on from that Capitol Hill group and into a more thoroughgoing enterprise. I had no idea what our Columbus group would look like once we started meeting or how all these different perspectives might come together, but I was excited to find out.

Our first session was at the University Club in downtown Columbus, at High Street and Main. Bill Lhota set it up for us. Rondo had been a member, going back a number of years, but by 1988, the place was open to the public. Bill told us about a private dining room they had in the back, and we thought that would be a good place to meet. It was, and we continued to meet at the University Club for about a year, because it was centrally located and nobody bothered us in the back room. It's no longer there. Over the years, we've closed down a number of well-known, landmark-type establishments, and the University Club was our first victim.

The thing I remember best about the first session is that we didn't really prepare anything. Ted was not yet in the habit of circulating a sheet of talking points and questions or assigning a passage for us to read. We just went in and read, and that's what I remember. That and the sticky rolls. The University Club was famous for its sticky rolls, the highlight of the menu.

Rondo was our designated reader in those days. Ted would tell him what to read, and he'd have at it. A lot of us didn't really know one another before that first meeting. We all had our own points of connection, our individual threads binding us to one or another, but we certainly weren't knitted together as a group. Rondo kind of knew Roach, and Roach and Rondo kind of knew Lhota. None of us really knew Ted except for Roach and Bob Davies, and I'd had just that one meeting with Ted and Roach at their church. Roach knew Bob Davies a little bit, but Dr. Davies came to us through Ted, so that was his connection. And I'd known Vogt for years through his work as a lobbyist, mostly in Washington. He knew a couple of the other guys, too, but only in a nodding acquaintance sort of way.

All these years later, no one can remember what we discussed at our inaugural meeting. There were a lot of getting-to-know-you elements in our first sessions. We were all still feeling one another out. I hadn't counted on this, because my experience in the Washington study group was that everyone kind of knew everyone else—by reputation, at least. I was the new guy, but I got the sense that everyone knew what to expect. Here, there were no expectations. And here, we'd all be the new guys, starting in together, linked by a desire to live better, richer, more meaningful lives. I don't think we really thought things through beyond that. We had no real idea how to get there from where we were starting out. We just trusted in Ted and each other and the Good Book to take us there.

As I've indicated, one of our group's recurring debates concerns the literal interpretation of these biblical texts, and we got into it almost immediately. As I said, I can't be sure that our very first discussion along these lines took place at our very first session, but I clearly recall touching on it in that back room at the University Club over sticky rolls, so it took root soon enough. Did these stories really happen, we took turns wondering as we felt one another out, or were they meant to be read as metaphor? Did Moses really hear the audible voice of God on that mountain, or was it more of an inner voice that somehow made it clear to him what God's plan was? We were sort of split on this, even then, and what's interesting is that the split seems to cut in entirely new ways each time out. One group will take a literal view one week, and then an entirely different group will take a literal view the next time around.

My view is, hey, it depends. How's that for a strong position? But it's never a slam dunk. I might have read a passage as a young man and had one interpretation, and I might go back to it again when I'm a little older and (presumably) wiser and take another view. The story of Job, for example, starts out as one of the most plausible, believable stories in the Bible, and I have no trouble believing wholeheartedly that it depicts a sequence of events that actually took place—that is, until I get to the very end. Everything works out great, Job gets his life back, and his faith is redeemed. It's such a clichéd storybook ending that it aggravated the living daylights out of me the first time I read it. Commentators have been back and forth on this for centuries, including some who argue that the ending is a later redaction to the original passage. It bugged me all over again when we read it for the first time as a group a couple of months into our study. It was like a sappy movie, I suggested, the way Job came out whole, and I put it to the group. What I got back was interesting. There was apparently a school of thought that the last chapter of the book of Job was written a long time after the initial text, and the more we talked about this, the more we seemed to come to a consensus. No, everything doesn't always work out in the end, and it might or might not have worked out here, but the great lesson is that it *can*. Believe in God, and anything can happen.

Rondo likes to bust my chops whenever I come down on the side of metaphor. He'll say, "Jack, if you don't believe this stuff, then why are you reading it?"

The thing about Rondo is that he'll take up either side of an argument, and I sometimes think he does so just to counter my view, so I'm quick to give it right back to him. "Red," I'll say, "the difference between you and me is I've actually read the Bible."

There's generally a good-natured back-and-forth, not just between Rondo and me but between and among all of us by this point, although from time to time, things can get a little heated. And yet even in these heated moments, there's a great respect and camaraderie around our table. No one's view is dismissed or discounted.

The story of Daniel and the lion's den offers a strong case in point. We struggled with this one the first time we read it as a group, and I think the reason we struggled was that we had our own difficulties imagining ourselves in Daniel's situation. It wasn't about whether this guy *really* stepped into the lion's den to demonstrate the courage of his faith. And it wasn't about how we might manage to confront some similar demons in the unlikely event that we ever found ourselves in such an unlikely scenario. Whether Daniel's three young friends Shadrach, Meshach, and Abednego were *really* cast into a fiery furnace by King Nebuchadnezzar because they would not bow down or worship his idol wasn't really at issue for us at that time in our lives.

At bottom, we all decided, the story was about whether faith-based courage had a real place in our lives at all, because back then, the talk among our group was that a lot of people seemed to want to run away from religion. They might go to church on Sunday, and they might worship in their own way at home, but they didn't want to go to a party and hear someone talking about God or Jesus or take a stand on an issue driven by their personal faith. It made them uncomfortable. Or maybe they were uncomfortable talking about it themselves in a public way. That's what this passage seemed to be about—the strength of one man to stand and make an argument for God. Let's face it, we have all felt the heat of that fiery furnace from time to time, and we have all been under attack from "beastly" individuals out to do us harm, but it's how we confront that heat and uphold our principles before our adversaries that defines us in the end.

We went around and around on this, until we finally ran out of time. We made a special point of keeping our first sessions to an hour, thinking that if we got in the habit of running on until we reached some kind of consensus we might never get back to work on those Monday afternoons. To this day, we're pretty good about breaking up at one o'clock, even if we're in the middle of it, but in the beginning, it was sometimes disconcerting to be debating against the clock. Over time, we got used to pulling the plug on our conversation and getting back to it at the next session—or not, as often happened.

Here, with Daniel, we surrounded the question of courage with our different points of view, and when we ran out of time, we were left to draw different pieces of strength and inspiration and to move on to the next thing. But we got back to it eventually. One of the great benefits of a long-running study group is that we reread these stories again and again, as we cycle through a second and a third time, and it just so happened that we found a shared through line on this when we read Daniel again about ten years after we first started meeting as a group, in the aftermath of the tragic school shootings at Columbine High School outside Denver. The shootings took place in April 1999, and our group got together a week or two later. The shootings were still very much in the news at that point and very much on our minds. Among the compelling story lines to emerge in the wake of that tragedy was the story of a young female victim. Reportedly, she was asked by one of the shooters if she believed in God. She replied, "You know I do." According to some accounts, she was further asked to renounce her belief or she would be shot, but she would not waver.

What strength! What conviction! What courage!

We considered the story of Daniel against the headlines of the day, and then we put the question to one another: If a gunman threatened to shoot us if we did not reject our faith, how would we respond? There were no easy answers to the moral dilemma we had set, and yet we kept coming back to the ghastly reality that this young woman in Colorado was promptly shot for her conviction. We sat in awe of this young woman as we considered her struggle alongside that of Daniel and his friends. Those stories were written thousands of years ago, and here we had a modern-day example of someone in a fiery furnace, except that her faith could not save her—at least, not on this earthly plane.

Yes, true courage only surfaces when you're put to a test, and we were only considering that test in theory. It wasn't real; it was metaphor. To that poor girl at that Colorado high school, though, the heat from the fiery furnace was all too real. And the difference was everything.

On first reading, the story of Daniel and his friends seemed to be about faith-based courage only. But as we looked at it again, we came to the shared view that it spilled over into a more general appraisal of courage—the courage to speak out when you see an injustice, the courage to risk life and limb to help another, the courage to risk all in service of an ideal. Having the courage of faith surely bleeds into every aspect of our lives. It's not merely about standing up for God; it's about standing up, period.

FIVE

Guiding Light

Here's something I didn't realize about our study until I sat down to write this book: Ted Smith keeps us on script and on task and on point.

How he's managed to do this has always been something of a marvel, because it appears to happen on its own. For one thing, we don't read the stories of the Old and New Testaments in any kind of order. Maybe Ted had some order in his head when we were starting out, but these days, he leaves it to us to chart our course of study. He'll say, "We're almost done with Romans, fellas. What do you want to read next?"

Every time, Roach says, "Let's do Revelation." This always gets a big laugh.

Every time, Ted says, "That's fine, but you'll have to get another minister." This always gets a bigger laugh.

Ted doesn't "do" Revelation, because it's a book about

what's going to happen at end times, and our group is more about what's happening in *our* time, so we give Revelation short shrift. It's just not Ted's thing, and for the most part, we're right with him on this. Everything else is up for grabs, though, and by this point, we've read each book at least a couple of times. We don't go in any set order, but we try not to repeat ourselves until we've hit all the high notes. We tend to stay away from the Psalms, although from time to time, we'll sneak one in there, as a kind of grace note. Usually, we'll tackle one chapter per session—sometimes less, sometimes more, depending on the material. But one chapter is about right, and what's astonishing to me is how we find something new each time out. There are lines in there you don't see the first time through that pop right out at you on a subsequent reading. Or there might be a sidebar-type story you're inclined to overlook that years later seems to get to the crux of the book's central theme. That's the great thing about the Bible. It's like holding up a mirror to the whole wide world and fitting yourself and your circumstance into the picture. Tilt the mirror one way, and you'll see one thing in the reflection; tilt it some other way, and you'll see something completely different.

We're like a democracy, and yet I imagine Ted is steering us in some subtle way. If we've been too long away from a book of the Old Testament, for instance, he might suggest that we return to it before tackling another apostle. If we've been too long on matters of personal growth, he might direct us toward more spiritual concerns. He's looking for balance and ballast, so he offers some gentle guidance when we need it.

Every now and then, the real world will encroach on the material but only in times of extremis. Mercifully, this doesn't happen too often. In fact, it happens rarely, but when it does, there's a special resonance to it, because whatever it is that is occupying our front-burner attention in our daily lives will invariably affect our reflection on eternity. A war, for one example. The attacks of September 11, 2001, for another. The massacre at Virginia Tech. We never drift into pop-culture news, because we're all in agreement that it has no place in our study, but we make room for matters of weight and moment, because invariably there'll be a kind of through line to those matters in whatever passage we happen to be reading.

In many ways, Ted's like our own preprogrammed GPS device, because he gets us where we're going. If it weren't for Ted, we'd lose all sense of direction, but he's got an uncanny ability to keep us on point and on course, while somehow managing to leave us thinking we're calling the shots. It's like spiritual jazz. I've been endlessly and wondrously surprised over the years at how Ted has us feeling as if our sessions are unfolding in a free-form, free-thinking way. He's blessed with a light touch and a firm hand—and we've been blessed in turn. Indeed, it's one of Ted's unique talents to be both informal and purposeful, and it's a great gift to our group, because the organic nature of our discussions is what keeps us thrumming.

Without it, I don't think we'd still be at it after all these years; with it, we're going strong.

By Ted's count, we lean away from his direction only three or four times a year—a remarkably low number when you think of the forceful personalities in the group and the depth and breadth of some of the issues we consider. We get into some deeply personal, deeply serious stuff, all linked in some way to our assigned text. Ted will make sure we cycle back to every book before long. It's the circle of life, as told through the greatest stories known to man. For a couple of years in there, we focused primarily on the individuals in these stories, instead of on the stories themselves. Rather than reaching for the moral of a particular story or considering the themes as they applied to our present-day circumstances, we looked at what we could learn from this person's life and from the choices he or she had to make along the way.

Whatever the focus, whatever the emphasis, we follow Ted's lead each time through. He has a good idea of which aspects of a particular passage might reverberate with our group and which might merit closer consideration. On second readings, we might take an alternative view of a familiar story, just to mix it up and keep things interesting. Or we might come to an entirely different shared view from the one we held on the first pass, because we're all at a whole other stage in our lives, coming at the material from an entirely new place, or we have learned more.

It comes down to perspective, wouldn't you agree? Where you stand and how you look back out at the world have everything to do with how open you are to the stories of the Bible and what those stories have to teach you. Or, how open we are to God's grace as he transforms us. On each pass, though, we're willing to be pointed in the right direction, and Ted provides a fine rudder.

Occasionally, though, we drift, and when we do, Ted is happy to drift along with us, until he finds the next opportunity to set us right. After one recent discussion, he let it be known that we didn't get to one of his key questions in our allotted time. He had wanted us to consider whether women were more spiritual than men, as evidenced by the passages we were reading in the New Testament as well as in our casual, present-day experiences. There might not have been a whole lot to it, except that he thought it was a good line to pursue.

"It's something I've always been interested in," Ted told me when I asked him to reflect on a time when our group didn't quite pick up on a suggested line of thought and moved instead in some other direction. "I thought we could wrestle with the nature of women, when it came to matters of God and religion. There were a lot of books or stories I could tie this to, because the Bible is filled with examples of women taking this kind of initiative. I wondered if there was something about the female gender that made them more open to this kind of thing."

And so, with a little prodding, we took it up at our next session, and what we got back was significant. Tim Bainbridge, our most recent "hire" at the time, didn't buy Ted's notion that women were more devout in the time of Jesus or even in more modern times. Those of us who'd been with Ted a number of years were disinclined to challenge him straightaway whenever he looked to jump-start a discussion with a sweeping generality. It's not that we were inclined to agree with him, either, but we'd learned to let Ted's observations marinate before biting into them. That was his style—and ours, in response. Very often, Ted's generalities would turn out to reveal a deeper truth upon reflection, but Tim probably hadn't picked up on this yet. Or maybe he had, and he just didn't see the argument. Besides, we'd all spent his first few months in the study encouraging Tim to speak freely, so he did just that.

He said, "Where does that come from? I don't think women are any more pious than men when it comes to this stuff."

"You don't think so?" Ted shot back with abundant good cheer. "Ask almost any clergyman where he gets the most active support for his programs, and he'll tell you it's among women. Look at the number of teachers in our church schools. The vast majority of them are women."

"You've been in those shoes," Tim allowed, conceding the point for the time being. "I haven't."

And then we were off and running, surrounding Ted's broad

thesis statement with our own points of view. Together, we offered our starting lineup of strong biblical women, beginning with Ruth, whose loyalty to her mother-in-law following her husband's death impressed our group as an act of true heroism and selfless devotion. Indeed, Ruth's words as she expressed her devotion to a woman who had told her to return to her own mother and remarry made such a strong impression that most of us could recite them from memory: "Wherever you go, I will go. Wherever you lodge, I will lodge. Your people shall be my people, and your God, my God. Where you die, I will die, and there will I be buried."

Our discussion continued from there, on to the woman who wiped the face of Jesus as He bled, the women who stood at the foot of His cross, the women who were dispatched to anoint His body.

We didn't want for examples, and now that Ted had us looking at these stories in just this way, we could see he was on to something. Women did appear to be cut a little differently when it came to spiritual matters, and we'd do well to take a look at it.

"But why?" Bob Blair wanted to know. "Why would women be more devout than men?"

"Maybe there's something about women that allows them to be less fearful," I tried, "and more willing to stand up on principle. Maybe it's how they're made."

Ted said, "It seems to me they might have a greater gift for devotion. Probably, they're more likely to be forgiving, although these days, they're also more likely to call for change. They're proactive about everything else, so why shouldn't they be proactive in their faith?"

Here, Tim brought us back to Ted's claim about women being the most active in churches, and he wanted to know if

they were "active" in terms of devotion or in terms of community building and outreach and that sort of thing.

"Aha!" Ted exclaimed, pleased that one of us had finally
taken his bait. "Maybe it's not about devotion per se. Maybe it's
not about faith or piety so much as it is devotion to an activity
or a responsibility. Or maybe it's just devotion to an ideal."

At this, Blair wanted to know what was behind the archaic
laws and customs that tended to require our religious leaders to
be men. "Why does the pope have to be a male?" he wondered.
"Where does it say that we will only follow men?"

"It's a carryover of the sexism that's existed for centuries,"
Ted explained.

"But that's wrong," Rondo weighed in. Rondo can be conspicuously silent for a long stretch, as if he's lying in the weeds,
and then he'll dive right into it. "It doesn't fit with the times,"
he said. "We follow women in all these other arenas. Why
shouldn't we follow them in the spiritual arena as well?"

"No, it doesn't fit with how we live," Blair agreed. "We
should speak out against it."

"And then what?" Rondo asked. "We speak out against it,
it's not gonna change anything."

"Well, why not?" Tim pressed. "The Episcopals have seen
the light on this. They now have women priests." He reminded
us that the presiding bishop of the Episcopal church was indeed
a woman—Katharine Jefferts Schori, elected in our own back-
yard, at the church's general convention in Columbus in June
2006. It was a neat connection, but the rest of us didn't see the
Catholic church changing its traditions on this anytime soon.

Rondo pointed out that there were now a great many female
rabbis in Jewish congregations around the world, but we noted
that the Orthodox Jewish community continued to prohibit
women from leading their congregations in prayer.

And on and on we went, with no consensus in sight—and no end but the clock that would tell us when our time was through. That's another thing we'd all picked up from Ted, the idea that we don't need to put any kind of exclamation point on things or wrap our discussions in a tidy bow of accord. We'll talk our way over, through, and around an issue, with Ted doing what he can to quarterback our conversation, and then we'll move on.

That's the fine rudder I wrote about earlier. We might shift with the winds or bend to the times, but Ted will find a way to keep us on course. And in those sessions when we can't help but drift, he'll lift that rudder and enjoy the slow ride.

Ted's favorite biblical story? I'll let him tell it.

"Jesus was out and about in His community," he says. "He was the talk of the countryside. Everywhere He went, He drew a crowd. It got so it was almost impossible to get in to see Him. He was a real tough ticket, if you will. A leper commented that there was such a crowd around Jesus when He went into this one building that there wasn't even room around the door or the windows. And it was at this moment that four men arrived on the scene carrying another man, a disabled man who couldn't possibly have gotten there by himself. By the time they got there, though, they couldn't get inside. The place was packed. The people who had assembled before these men and their friend weren't about to give up their spots, not even for a man who was paralyzed. They were thinking, *Hey, if you wanted to be here, you should have gotten here early, like we did.*

"But the four men would not be turned away. They had come a long way. They would do whatever it took to get their friend inside. They also sought a way in for themselves, because they wanted to see what was going on, but they were mostly concerned about their buddy. He had no other way of getting there without the kindness and cooperation of his able-bodied companions. Plus, he seemed to need to be there in a way the other four did not. They were already men of faith, and plenty, while this paralyzed man was filled with doubt and worry. So what did they do? Well, the four able-bodied men climbed up onto the roof and disassembled part of the roof, which was made of thatch, and then they hoisted the paralyzed fellow up to the roof so they could lower him down through the opening. That had to be an interesting scene. And the record said that because of their great faith and great determination, this paralyzed fellow would be able to walk home.

"Quite a story, don't you think? Obviously, these four guys would have liked to have been inside that house. They would have liked box seats, too. But instead of just elbowing their way in like everybody else, they'd walked clear across town to collect their friend, who would have missed out entirely without their dedication and devotion. And what did they get for their efforts? Well, they were nearly turned away, and then they climbed up onto that roof and hoisted this fellow right up there with them, they were so determined. There was some protestation from the guy who owned the house, of course, when they were tearing his roof apart, but they kept at it. I imagine they had some trouble at first, lowering their friend through the opening they'd made, but they found a way. I can close my eyes and see one of them taking off to try to find some ropes to tie to the corners of the stretcher or rig some sort of pulley. I just love how creative these men were, how resourceful. Their devotion, their dedication . . . it was all quite remarkable, really. And as a result, this guy's life was forever changed. He could walk home after all.

"To be honest, I've never really thought about picking out a favorite passage, but I guess this would have to be it. It's from the book of Mark, and it offers a powerful lesson. It has all the elements. And the best part is that you have all these people, with all this powerful motivation. Sometimes conflicting motivation. You know, the village is crowded with motivation. Everybody wanted to get in to have an audience with Jesus Christ. It was the big excitement in the community. People far and wide were talking about it. But these four guys, with their superior motivation, headed off in a completely opposite direction. They went against the crowd. They did whatever they could to bring their great friend to Jesus, a man who by all accounts was a man of no great faith. But their conviction was such that they could only act in this selfless way. Nothing was more important than the chance to bring their friend to Jesus. They probably gave up a day of work to help out their buddy, and they certainly gave up their own chance to get inside, and we can all draw our own inspiration from that."

As I listened to Ted lay out the particulars of this story from Mark, I couldn't help but see a link to the role Ted plays in our study. It put me in mind of the way he had us look at the individuals in these stories and not just at the stories themselves, and I began to see how Ted's firm hand in even our loosest, most casual discussions has kept us on a sure and steady course. I've taken to calling him the Holy Man among our group. It's an affectionate nickname I offer with great reverence and respect, and he doesn't seem to mind it, so I plan on wearing it out—because this, too, is an outgrowth of the way Ted has encouraged us to pursue this study. He's made it so that it's about relationships as much as about spirituality. It's not about him. It's not about any set agenda. It's about pushing ourselves to make the most of our time on this earth so that we can make the most of our eternity. It's about knitting us together, as well.

I hadn't known Ted going into this enterprise, but I now count him among my closest friends. The rest of the guys in the study think of him the same way, so here he is, filling something like the same role in our lives as these four men who carried their friend through that crowd on his stretcher and onto that roof. No, we're not exactly helpless, like the disabled man on the stretcher in Ted's favorite tale. And no, we're not exactly wandering in the wilderness in terms of our faith, but we're all in need of an assist, and that's what Ted provides for us, in subtle ways and in obvious ways.

He brings us to Jesus, my friend Ted the Holy Man. Sometimes, there's even heavy lifting. The difference is that we match him step for step along the way.

Ask Ted, and he'll tell you that the central, abiding element of our study is faith. His. Ours. The faith of mankind in general. "It's the key to what we do," he reflects, "because it's the key to the whole Book, from Genesis clear through to the last book of the New Testament. And yet faith and belief are two very different concepts in the Bible, just as they represent two different concepts in our lives."

A great many people use those terms interchangeably, but that's a mistake, if you ask Ted. According to the Holy Man, belief is coming to understand facts and assessing a situation and being able to know it or touch it or see it yourself. "Faith is a choice," he maintains. "It's an act. You don't arrive at faith because you'd be a fool if you don't subscribe to this or that notion. Belief is what happens when the facts are laid out for you, and it's clear you'll be a fool if you don't believe. Clearly, if it's incontrovertible fact, you've got to believe. That's the way the word is used, from Genesis to Revelation, whereas *faith* is used differently. And it was Abraham's faith that cast him as a friend to God. Absolutely, it was faith. He ventured out to Iraq, to Iran, all the way to Palestine. It's described as an act of faith on his part. He's described as a man of faith. Then, in the Old Testament, their principal characteristic that made them noteworthy was faith. It was not simply their conformity to the Big Ten. It was not what they came to believe. It was their faith, and it's named many, many times. Moses is identified that way, and Noah. David is described that way as well. The key, it seems to be, in identifying all those guys, they were described as men of faith.

"That's how I'd describe these guys in the study," Ted says, shifting gears, turning his attention to the here and now. "When they came and asked me to take this on, it was a very challenging opportunity. I realized it was something I'd always wanted to do, but I hadn't really thought about it. I was satisfied in the work I was doing in my church, but this was different. There was something uniquely valuable in what these guys were trying to do, something separate and apart from what I was doing with my parishioners. We ran groups in my church, of course, and there was great value in that as well, but John and Roach and these guys were real hard chargers, they had their own ideas, and I could either sign on to them or step aside."

What I responded to in Ted from the very beginning was his pursuit of the real, and I believe it's what he responded to in us. It's what I'd been after since I climbed through that window Stu Boehmig told me about just after my parents' death. It's what Bob Roach had been looking for when we locked heads over that Christmas keg. We were out to separate the rhetoric from the authentic, and it's been a boon and a blessing that this has been Ted's approach as well—not just for Roach and me but for all of us, because we're mostly reaching for the same things, and what we're mostly reaching for is the freedom to chase our own destinies. That's what faith can do for you. It frees you up to anticipate the next world, and when you focus in on eternity, you can see things a whole lot more clearly in this world.

Ted talks all the time about a desire to grab on to whatever is fundamentally real or fundamentally true in life. "If that's the existence of a supreme being," he explains, "and if that's fundamentally true and reliable as it relates to our time on this earth, then that becomes our bottom line."

The study, he says, is not *just* about the Book. To a guy like Ted, there's a whole lot about life and spirituality that's not in the Book, but it stands as a foundation just the same. It's front and center and all around, and the bottom line for Ted has been to help us with our shared search for meaning and our deepening relationships with God. If He's here, what does He expect of us? What do we expect in return? Every once in a while, we're like Pink Floyd; we catch ourselves asking, "Is there anybody out there?" Ted's cut the same way. He's quick to admit it, in fact, and I don't know too many ministers who'd be so candid about their occasional uncertainties. Men of God are supposed to be resolute in their faith, yet Ted never lets us forget that they're also men. They're human. Life can't help but push us to uncertainty, and when that happens, we've got the Good Book to pull us back.

And one another.

And Ted.

We've been at it for a good, long while by this point—and, God willing, we'll be at it a while longer.

"It hasn't been twenty years," Ted says. "It's been a week. OK, maybe two weeks. But twenty years? No, sir. No chance. Because it's a living, vital, vibrant thing. It can't get old."

SIX

Up and Running

W E FOUND OUR STRIDE SOON ENOUGH. AS A GROUP, WE weren't exactly as focused as I would have hoped heading into our first session, but each time out, we could see a deepening commitment. Each time out, we became more and more comfortable with one another, more and more excited about what we could accomplish on our shared search for meaning, more and more as if we were on to something.

Our first sessions were hit-or-miss. Ted started out with a fairly firm hand on our discussions. He'd run Bible studies before, of course, and there was no reason to think ours would be different, at least not in terms of structure or stricture, but he'd liked the enthusiasm Roach and I had demonstrated when we went to see him in his office, and he was excited to have his buddy Bob Davies on board. Yet when the gun finally went off and we looked to hit the ground running, I think we all went into default mode. We reached for what we knew, bits and pieces of every other study group that had left us wanting something different, something more.

This was most noticeable in the role we'd set aside for Ted, because it fell to him to establish a tone, and I think we all underestimated how difficult that would be. Roach and I had been so busy telling Ted the kind of group we really *didn't* want that we never took the time to articulate what kind of group we really *did* want, so we were all figuring it out as we went along. And that was right and good and appropriate, because there was nothing wrong with any of these other groups that had left us wanting. Together, though, we were reaching for something more.

Ted's approach made sense. It fit. Traditionally, a minister assigned to lead a group of this kind did so from on high. In church basements and meeting rooms around the country, this was how it was done. There was a built-in authoritarian aspect to the role, so our first sessions felt a little bit as if they were being led by a teacher instead of being steered and gently influenced by a more experienced, more knowledgeable hand. It was a small distinction, to be sure, but it was all-important. I didn't want to feel that I was being *led* so much as I was being *guided*. Instead of feeling *pushed*, I wanted to feel *accompanied*. And even with that good guidance, in that good company, I wanted to be able to head down a wrong road or two and see where it took us.

Make no mistake, Tom Barrett did a great job at the helm of my D.C. study group, but there was no underpinning of real fellowship in that group. To this day, I consider Tom a true friend, and I'm endlessly impressed at the way he's nourished that Capitol Hill group over the years, but what was missing in it for me was a sense of collective purpose. Tom kept pushing us to "keep it real," but it was a slog. The realities of our lives kept getting in the way. We were all elected officials, after all, traveling back and forth between Washington and our home districts, and the study was necessarily set up so we could all come and go as our busy schedules allowed. None of us really had any time for fellowship or forging new friendships. What this meant, in practice, was that we were never able to feel as if we were in this thing together, powering through the lessons of the Book in search of common ground and sure footing, standing as one another's moral compass, if you will.

For the most part, the participants in the D.C. study were good, caring guys, but it came to feel as if we were going through the motions—not together so much as in one another's midst. There was some real reflection, but we were off on our separate journeys. Tom did what he could to lead us, but it must have been tough to lead such a group of headstrong, willful, ambitious men—and we weren't about to be guided, either.

There's a great line you hear all the time when you live and work in Washington: "If you want a friend in D.C., buy a dog." For whatever reason, people just don't have the time or the inclination to form real friendships, or they just don't see the need. And yet, despite that mind-set, Tom brought to light some amazing biblical truths and tied a great many passages to what we were going through in our lives and careers. Ultimately, though, the bonds of intimacy and friendship just weren't there, and that was at least a part of what I was looking for.

So where did that leave us in the back room at the University Club, trying not to fill up on sticky rolls? For the time being, we could only flounder and retrace our steps, and we did so in these time-honored ways. Yeah, it fit, but only in the sense that a new pair of jeans might fit; it took a while for us to wear it in and start to feel comfortable.

It wasn't just Ted looking to build this upstart Columbus study on familiar ground. It was all of us, in our own ways. We could only reach for what we knew, and so we reached and hoped that what came back had a little more heft to it than what we'd drawn before. Personally, I was just thrilled that we'd gotten this group off the ground at all. It didn't matter at the outset that the ground was familiar; it only mattered that we were walking it. And besides, I'd found enough to like about Ted in our first few conversations to know that we could evolve into the sort of study I'd imagined.

It'd just take a little time, that's all.

One of the first tweaks we thought to make as a group was in our personnel. A couple of months in, we started to realize that we needed another participant or two to shore up our ranks. Seven, it turned out, was an impractical number. We had thought it would be just right, or just shy of just right, but as it was playing out, we didn't have a deep enough bench to compensate for the twists and turns in our busy schedules. We were finding that one or two of our group were almost always being pulled away to attend some meeting or deal with a professional emergency, which in turn pulled some of the vibrancy from our sessions. It was inevitable and unavoidable, but it was nevertheless a drag on our momentum. And yet our head count wasn't the only drag; even when our sessions were fully attended, it felt as if we could use another voice or two in the chorus to enrich the conversation.

And so, since we were meeting on Monday afternoons, our very first Tuesday-morning-quarterback sessions had to do with bringing on another few members. I stayed late a time or two to discuss this with Roach and Ted and a few others and to kick around some other ways we might enhance the group. What was missing, we all agreed, was another few kindred spirits.

Not incidentally, these postgame, poststudy analysis sessions were a key to our development at the outset. Remember, it wasn't so easy for us to plug in to one another during the week and keep connected the way we do today. Our idea of high-tech communication back then was beepers and answering machines, so we took full advantage of our limited time together to iron out some of these wrinkles. We did this in a variety of informal, impromptu ways. We stayed on in the back room at the University Club or lingered in the parking lot out front. Roach had some ideas whenever we got together on this. Ted did, too. And after a couple of months, we were all casting about for friends and acquaintances we could bring in.

Now that we were a going concern, it wasn't just up to Roach or me to decide who would be invited in. Come to think of it, we never really discussed any criteria for admitting new members or any ground rules for other changes we might make as we were taking shape. We just figured this stuff would take care of itself—and, happily, it did. The changes in Ted's approach, for example, came about in a natural way. He was smart enough to read the room and see that he could get more out of us with a more relaxed approach, so he relaxed. Plain and simple. He saw that we were more engaged, more in tune with one another when the discussion was more informal, so he loosened his collar, so to speak, and changed things up.

Here's a great example of how Ted looked to retrofit his style to our group. He got in the habit early on of preparing wonderful talking-point sheets for us, which would list certain questions he wanted us to consider as we did our assigned reading before each study, and it's a habit he's kept up to this day. Even now, when he could zap these sheets to us electronically, he types them up, prints them out, and drops them in the mail. At the other end, we take our hard copies, mark them up by hand, and stuff them into our pockets on our way to the session. It's basic—a throwback, really—and yet, even here, I believe the Holy Man knows what he's doing. So much of what we read and write these days is disposable. So much of what we talk about and consider is forgettable. It's one of the sad outgrowths of our information age, the way all these texts and e-mails and status updates exist in the ether, in the moment, in some sort of ephemeral way. We hit our Send buttons without a careful thought, or, at the other end, we hit Delete before giving ourselves a chance to think things through. The idea is that technology is supposed to improve the ways we communicate, and it does, but it also cheapens some of our basic human interactions, and Ted has picked up on this. He's a smart guy. He recognizes that sending us these hard copies and forcing us to spend some time with the material in this more concrete way lets us come to the study with a little more depth and clarity to our thoughts.

All of that came later, of course. We evolved with the times—or against the times. (Despite them, even.) However, the first quantifiable adjustment to our setup was in number. We recognized this right away, and yet we were in no hurry to grow the group. We knew that personal chemistry, character, trustworthiness, and all those other intangible elements would be critical to our ongoing efforts, so we moved carefully. We were knee-deep in personal and intimate conversations, so we couldn't reach out to just anybody to fill out our ranks. Over the course of our first year or so, we considered a bunch of prospects, but we never really found the right guy. Or when we did find the right guy, he wasn't all that interested. Bob Blair, who'd eventually sign on to the enterprise seventeen years later, didn't have any interest the first couple of times I approached him. I'd known Blair since my days in the state legislature. Actually, since day one. He was the first friend I made when I went to work in the Ohio Senate, and right away, he became like an older brother to me. We kept connected over the years, even after I went to Congress, and when I was back home in Columbus, I told Blair what we were up to with this group. He was intrigued enough to ask how things were going from time to time, but he wasn't a particularly spiritual guy back then. He just didn't have any interest, but I vowed to keep at him.

My pursuit of Blair to join our ranks offers a compelling case in point. For good or ill, most of the recruiting fell to me, and I came to see it as an art, not a science. I developed a feel for it over time. There were certain givens. You don't want someone to be a disruptive force. You want someone who is open to the power of God, with a basic curiosity regarding eternity. Someone with a clear fit on what constitutes "life" or "living." I'm in this thing because I have an interest in peering through that window Stu Boehmig opened for me after my parents' death. The other guys have their own versions of the same interest, and I have to think that anyone else who signs on with us will as well.

Another given is that whoever it is has to fit in with the rest of the group. Here, we're mostly going on gut, but we haven't been wrong yet. It's just like putting together any other group of people, for any other reason. You have to get along. We look only to people of character. Everybody in our group is a fine person. Everybody in our group is selfless. Everybody digs deep and gives back.

And above all, we need someone we can trust. Throw in with us, and you need to know how to keep your mouth shut, because we talk about all kinds of intimate, personal stuff—

stuff that's not for this book and not for any discussion outside the bounds of our sessions. The folks on my campaign staff have an expression for conversations and inside information that can never be made public: "It stays in the lodge." That's how we feel in our group, and it's not because we're revealing anything of note or moment or consequence, except for little pieces of ourselves that we don't care to trot out for public inspection. Our hopes and fears and spiritual concerns are just that—*ours*. If we choose to share them with someone outside our group, that's up to us, but if one of our guys shares a doubt or a crisis or a moral dilemma, it can't leave the lodge. No, sir.

I don't pay much attention to anyone's denomination or affiliation. Heck, I don't pay it any attention at all. None of us does. It's just not important. We might kid one another from time to time, dismissing a certain type of behavior as typical of this or that group, but I don't see any fundamental differences among these many ideologies. Lutheran, Baptist, Protestant, Catholic . . . we're all cut from the same cloth. We're all Christians at heart. I happen to have been raised in a Catholic church, so there's always going to be a part of me that considers myself a Catholic. Ted is a Methodist. Roach is a Methodist, too, and I know that only because he belongs to Ted's church. Other than that, I honestly couldn't tell you who stands in what line. Some of our guys weren't even affiliated with any church when they signed on with us, and that's all right, too. Whatever works, is how I look at it—whatever gets and keeps you closer to God.

I worship in an Anglican church because I want to get Communion every Sunday. That's not always the case in some of the other churches, but other than that, I'd be comfortable almost anywhere. I know a lot of people don't feel that way, and I respect that, but for a lot of people, church is also about community and fellowship. That's not me. When I worship in church, it's a very private matter—I guess because I'm such a public person in every other aspect of my life. I don't go to church suppers or pancake breakfasts or various social events. That's not why I go to church. I go simply to carve out a special pocket of time in my crazy, busy week to dwell in the presence of God and to receive Communion. It's important to me. I don't even feel that I need to pray with my family, at least not all the time. My daughters go to a Christian school, and I'm very proud of the fact that they have both come to know the Lord. They have an age-appropriate understanding of what God is about, and that's reinforced for them every day at school, so I don't make them come to church with me on Sunday mornings. They can join me if they want, but I don't force it on them, and it doesn't seem to me that they're missing out. My wife, Karen, knows the Lord. She worships on her own, in a variety of ways, and a lot of times, she just plain needs a break on Sunday mornings, after getting up early all week and chasing after our girls. Don't misunderstand me, I love it when my family joins me, but I also love it when they don't, because I find great strength and comfort in knowing that my girls are sleeping peacefully at home, cloaked in God's embrace and in my own as well.

My Bible study guys and I all worship in our own ways. Some of us don't actively *worship* at all, but that wouldn't necessarily exclude you from our group. As long as your heart's in the right place and you're open to the wondrous possibilities of eternity and spirituality, we might just find a place for you. One guy who didn't have an obvious interest in any type of organized religion was Mark Bechtel, a doctor I had come to know back home. Mark was one of the first doctors in the country to link the developing AIDS epidemic to a skin rash doctors were starting to see in certain parts of Africa. Some of the very first cases in the United States were turning up in and around Columbus all the way back in 1980, before the disease even had a name. Mark was still doing his training during this period, and he saw a patient with an unusual rash of purple spots who eventually developed pneumonia and died. He wrote it up in one of the journals and got a lot of attention for it, so much so that he started giving interviews about the disease and its implications.

Mark was really out in front on this as a young doctor. He appeared on one religious cable station in Columbus, and the reporter thought he was talking about the Ayd's diet plan, which was a popular nutritional supplement at the time. The reporter was asking questions like "Dr. Bechtel, how much weight do you expect patients to lose with Ayd's?" And Mark matter-of-factly said, "Most of our patients lose about twenty pounds before they die." And the interviewer said, "What, people die from Ayd's?" And Mark said, "So far as we know, everyone will eventually die from AIDS." It was such a colossal misunderstanding, and it could have been an absurdly funny Abbott and Costello routine if it wasn't so deadly serious.

Mark was my doctor. That's how we met. He tells the story now that the first time he drew blood from me, I said, "If this hurts, I'll raise your taxes."

I don't remember that, but it's probably true. It sounds like me, and Mark's got a terrific memory.

What I liked about Mark was that he was one of the most selfless people I'd ever met. He's a real servant—he still makes house calls. And yet, for all his care and boundless concern for his patients, I never knew him as a man of faith. He belonged to a church, but he never went. His wife took his two young kids. For some reason, I thought Mark would be a great addition to the study group and, as important, that the study would be a great benefit to him as well.

We became friends, and I told him what we were doing over at the University Club. His interest was piqued—or so I thought. We talked about it a little more. Granted, I did most of the talking, but Mark asked some probing, relevant questions. He reminded me of myself, when I'd first decided to pursue that D.C. study group. Basically, he wanted to know if what we were after was *real* or *routine*.

Now, all these years later, Mark confesses that he wasn't looking for spiritual guidance as much as friendship. He also confesses that he wasn't all that interested in what we were doing, not at first. He told me recently that the only reason he ultimately decided to come to one of our sessions was that I'd badgered him into it. He was just trying to be polite, and he'd run out of excuses. Here I'd been thinking we'd somehow tapped into Mark's hidden desire to connect with the Big Guy, when in truth he couldn't keep putting me off. Religion wasn't any kind of big deal to him. It is now, way up there on his long list of priorities, but he didn't think he had time for it in those days. He didn't think he had the head for it, either. He also didn't have time for any social pursuits outside work, and he thought this group might be a good way to plug some of those holes. He was particularly intrigued by the idea of getting to know Dr. Davies, another one of our original members, whom Mark knew by reputation as one of the most well-respected doctors in the state. The connection, he thought, couldn't hurt.

That put our group at eight, but we weren't done yet.

Mark Bechtel still remembers his first session all these years later. He didn't know what to expect. Despite all of his questions and due diligence, a part of him thought he'd find some Bible-thumping evangelicals, celebrating Jesus and whooping it up in the back room at the University Club, but he got us instead, a group of hardworking professional men, keenly interested in learning how to integrate the word of God and the stories of the Bible into their daily lives.

What he didn't find, unfortunately, was me. I'd been waving our flag and badgering him to join our group, and then I was called to Washington at the last minute and couldn't make it to Mark's first session. How's that for a rotten sales job? I'd managed to bring him to the door, but I couldn't hold it open for him. I felt just terrible about it. The poor guy sat at that table, and he didn't know anybody, so he was a little uncomfortable. He shouldn't have been surprised by what he found, though, because I'm sure the group came across as advertised. They were reading Romans that day, Mark recalls, and he'd done the reading and considered Ted's questions going in, but he didn't say anything. He just sat and listened—and probably wondered what the heck he'd just gotten himself into.

"They couldn't have been nicer or more welcoming," he says, "so it wasn't that, but I had no frame of reference for what these guys were doing. And part of the reason for that was that this type of thing just wasn't on my radar at all. Even though I'd grown up in the Presbyterian church, we never really discussed religion at home, and once I started college, I almost set it aside. It was a part of me, and then it wasn't. I'd still go to the chapel from time to time, just to help me keep my focus, but certainly not on any kind of regular basis. It wasn't a priority, but then, my first Christmas away from home, I started really feeling this void. I was really struggling. I thought I needed the time to study for my exams, so I stayed in the dorm, and there was hardly anyone around. I listened to a lot of Christmas music on the radio, and it helped me to focus. I also started praying. It wasn't something I thought about consciously, I just found myself praying. You know, for the strength to succeed, to persevere, to do well enough on my exams that I could get into medical school. The usual stuff. And then, when all those prayers were answered for me, I drifted away. I became so busy I didn't think I had time for this sort of thing."

And yet "this sort of thing" was elemental for the six other guys huddled around Mark that first Monday afternoon, and he was inspired by their passion, their insights, their dedication. (Lord knows, if I'd been there that Monday, I might have turned him off to the whole deal!) He decided then and there to make it elemental for him as well.

We made two other early additions to the group, which helped to soften the blow of an early defection. Bill Lhota drifted away from us after a short time, owing mostly to his busy, unpredictable schedule. As an executive in a big company, he told us he was finding it increasingly difficult to peel away from work on Monday afternoons. I was sad to see Bill go, because I had a lot of admiration for him. He was a real straight shooter, and we needed his kind of candor, but there was no twisting his arm, so it appeared we had an open seat. None of us felt the need to scramble to fill it, but it was generally agreed that we would all be on the lookout for someone who might fit into our mix.

I found a strong candidate soon enough: Bob McQuaid. We all called him Coach, to avoid confusion with our other Bobs. I met this Bob at the gym, and back in the early 1990s, when you pumped iron on a regular basis with the same group of guys, you developed real friendships. Real *guy's guy* sort of friendships. You talked about anything and everything or nothing much at all. These days, everyone in my gym has stringy white earbuds running from their iPods into their heads, discouraging conversation, but that wasn't the case twenty years ago. Back then, we used to spot each other and talk, and every once in a while, we'd find ourselves drifting into the spiritual realm. No, I don't wander past all the weights and machines, mumbling to myself about God and religion or talking to every lost soul about Bible study, but when you're off in search of like-minded souls, you tend to develop a kind of radar for people of faith.

Bob McQuaid was a tough guy with a big heart, from a big blue-collar family. Lots of brothers and sisters. Hardworking, God-fearing parents. Solid family values across the board. He was raised Catholic, but, like me, he found his early churchgoing experiences more rooted in rote than in deep-seated meaning. Without really realizing it, he was looking for something more.

Coach was a fundamentally good guy, as comfortable talking sports or nutritional supplements as anything else. He sold cars for a living, but we never really talked about work while he pounded the iron and laughed at my weak efforts to keep pace. "Go hard or go home!" he used to yell at me when we worked out together, and I started to think those words could apply to our approach in the study. I found myself thinking he'd be a great fit with our group.

The other guys took to Coach right away, as I knew they would. In fact, he became especially close to Dick Vogt, and that friendship has been strengthened over the years. That's how it seems to happen in our group. Certain guys hit it off. I don't know how or why, but it happens. We all get along around the table, and we all have a great deal of respect and admiration for one another, but these separate extracurricular friendships invariably develop out of the study and that's what happened with these two guys. They just clicked.

Craig MacDonald was another guy I knew around town.

Like Rondo, he was one of those guys who got along with just about everybody. He was a graduate of the U.S. Air Force Academy, with a great scientific mind, not the sort of fellow you'd expect to throw in on a Bible study group, and yet he fit himself right in. We'd played a lot of golf together, and I've always felt you can tell a lot about a man by the way he plays a round of golf. Craig was honest and focused and thorough, on the course and in the study group. He was a great athlete, which, of course, frustrated me no end when I was out on the course with him, but unlike a lot of golfers I know with God-given ability, he didn't carry himself with any arrogance or bluster when he played. He was patient and humble and decent, qualities I thought would serve him well around our table.

Craig worked for Battelle Memorial Institute, one of the leading research-and-development labs in the country, with lasers and robots and all sorts of high-tech stuff. He had a curious, probing mind, which I knew would be an asset to our study group if he signed on. He was a man of great depth and character. I was enormously fond of him and thrilled when he agreed to give us a try.

With Bill Lhota gone and these two strong additions in Coach and Craig, that put us at nine members. I remember going to Mark Bechtel's office one afternoon, maybe four or five years after he'd joined the group and our new and improved lineup had begun to have a little history behind it. I wanted to know how things were going for him and if the group was turning out to be everything he expected, and his answer surprised me.

He said, "John, I deal with life-and-death circumstances all the time. That was the case before I joined the group, and I never really knew how to deal with it. It was always emotional, and I was always compassionate, but now I'm able to help these families through difficult transitions in ways I could have never imagined. I went into this thing to maybe rekindle my faith and maybe make some new friends, but it's been so much more than that. Almost from the very beginning, it's been so much more than that."

Then he told me a very moving story about a man he'd just helped at the hospital. The poor fellow was grieving over a loved one's illness, and Mark took the time to reach out to him. He said, "Would you like me to take you to the hospital chapel?" The man was willing to be led, and the two men sat and prayed together for a few meaningful moments. As Mark shared the story with me, I marveled at the transformation in my good friend. Years ago, it would have never occurred to him to guide a patient or a grieving family member to prayer; it simply wasn't part of his worldview. And yet here he was now, a man of science who had also made room in his heart for hope and faith and eternity.

Indeed, that's been one of the neat by-products of our time together in the study. It's reawakened our faith as individuals. We're there every other Monday afternoon, pursuing this stuff in an intellectual way, forging all these intimate friendships, and finding wonderful points of connection between the Good Book and our crazy, hectic lives, but it's filled our hearts and our souls along the way. Quite a few of us had fallen out of the habit of attending church with any regularity before starting in with this group, but now most of us go every Sunday. We go for our own reasons, I guess. Part of the reason I go is to set a positive example for my children, but I remind them that church is not the only place God lives for me. That's not where I feel closest to Him. I go to pay respect to Him. I go to honor Him, and to worship Him. I go because it's a place of peace and quiet and solemnity, offering a glorious point of pause to the rest of the week.

I don't go looking for stimulation or uplift, even if they sometimes find me anyway. But it doesn't matter either way, because I know I'll get that from my Bible guys, every other Monday afternoon.

SEVEN

The End of Something

I SUPPOSE IT WAS TO BE EXPECTED THAT A GROUP OF MIDDLE-aged men coming together to mull and mirror the human condition might experience its share of heartache and grief over the years, but no one could have predicted it would find us so soon or so suddenly.

Mark Bechtel was the first to pick up on what happened, in a sidelong way. He went to a football game with his son on a rainy Friday night in 2001. When they got home, they flipped on the late local news, hoping to see a report from the game they'd just attended. Instead, they came across a breaking story about the crash of a small plane that had taken off that night from nearby Don Scott Field and was headed for upstate New York. No other details were given, and Mark didn't really think anything of it. He just thought, *Oh, that's horrible*, and filed it alongside all the other horrible things he'd seen and heard that week, that month, that year.

The next morning, though, Ted called each one of us in turn. Mark had never heard Ted so distraught, so shaken. I'd never heard him that way, either. He's usually so thoughtful and precise in his choice of words, but here he was fumbling, tentative. His voice was thick with emotion. I immediately knew something was horribly wrong.

What was wrong was this: Dr. Bob Davies had been flying that small plane. There was a terrible, violent storm, and he crashed in a field just outside Syracuse, New York. His wife had been on board. There were no survivors.

It was such a devastating piece of news, and it found us all in the wake of the September 11 attacks, so we were already raw and frazzled and emotionally drained. To lose someone so close so soon after a national tragedy was enough to cast men of faith into a sea of doubt. All of a sudden, the world didn't make a whole lot of sense. All of a sudden, the ground at our feet seemed shaky. Already, there had been a pall over our discussions, as we tried to make sense of those planes flying into those buildings, of all those lives lost. Typically, we try not to let the news of the day seep into the study group. We put up a kind of spiritual firewall and make a conscious effort to shut out the headlines, because our discussions are meant to be timeless, but that was impossible right after September 11. We continued with our readings and our discussion, but our talk was tinged with sorrow and worry. And now we'd struggle to make sense of another plane falling from the sky—this one with our fellow Bible guy and his wife on board.

Tell me, how do you make sense of *that*?

Flying had been a very big part of Dr. Davies's life. It fit right in with his larger-than-life persona, and it's what allowed him to participate in the study group. As I wrote earlier, Dr. Davies flew to the sessions every other week from his home in Troy, about eighty miles west of Columbus. He made a Herculean effort to participate. In fact, the "commute" was usually our first line of small talk as we settled into our seats. Dr. Davies was very often one of the first there, because he didn't have to deal with such mundane aspects of life as traffic, and we'd always ask if it was good flying weather or if he'd made good time. His routine was to touch down at a local commuter airport and rent a car for the short drive to the restaurant. Or sometimes Ted would meet Dr. Davies and give him a ride. And now the very plane that had been such a focus of Dr. Davies's life and a symbol of his devotion to our Bible studies had crashed, and we were left to wonder what had happened. And why.

We were reeling, even as we tried to stay the course, persevere in the study group, and continue as before. For the time being, at least, that seemed to be the plan; no one suggested otherwise. We'd been at this thing for more than a dozen years by this point, and we'd never missed a session. To be sure, the group had been thinly attended from time to time, owing to our occasionally busy schedules. We'd been sometimes distracted by the news of the day in such a way that we never quite made it to Ted's agenda or to the assigned reading. We'd been nearly shut down by bad weather. But we'd never canceled a session, and there was no reason to think we would do so now.

Ted hadn't mentioned anything of the sort when he called with the news. If it was something he wanted to do, we would have certainly honored that, because Ted was Dr. Davies's closest friend in the group. We were all prepared to follow his lead. He was really grieving; he and Bob were best friends. Their friendship preceded the study group—it transcended it, you could say. They spoke all the time during the week, and their wives had been fond of each other as well. Ted was really shaken up. Years later, he told me it was like losing a brother.

We were all shocked and saddened, but the news took its time sinking in. Rondo remembers getting the call from Ted, setting the phone down, and wondering if what he'd just heard could possibly be true. It was such a surreal, otherworldly bulletin that a part of him thought there had to be some other explanation for it. Bob Roach says he sat quietly by himself for the longest time after Ted's call, thinking how much Dr. Davies had loved flying that plane. It had been his joy, his release. The two of them had been the only guys in the study who'd known Ted going in, so they had a little more history, a little more connective tissue, than the rest of us.

Dick Vogt was probably the most pragmatic of our group, and he also remembers sitting still and silent for the longest while after hanging up the phone.

I was on the road, traveling back from giving a speech, and I think the first thing I did after I got off the phone with Ted was to call Karen. I can't be certain, though. I remember making that call, but I can't be sure that it was the very next thing I did. It's possible that I prayed. It's also possible that I was pulled away on some other call or dragged into a meeting or distracted by some pressing matter. In any case, I reached out to Karen as soon as I could. I told her the news, but that's not really why I called. I just wanted to hear her voice and plug back into a world that made sense, to reestablish some type of firm footing.

As the details became clear, I couldn't shake the picture I had of Dr. Davies in his final moments—an accomplished, confident, resourceful man, unable to fly his plane through the storm, knowing there was no way out for him and his lovely wife. This was a guy who could do anything, and yet he couldn't get control over that machine. It was such a haunting picture, and it must have been such an agonizing moment, and I couldn't shake it.

We were all shaken by Dr. Davies's death, but as we moved forward from it, I realized that there had been a real distance between us. Maybe *distance* is the wrong word, but we hadn't been especially close. I'd had a different sort of relationship with Dr. Davies than I had with the other guys in the group. I respected his intellect, I valued his opinion, I enjoyed his company, and I considered his strongly held points of view. But we never really socialized, mostly because he lived so far away. He was never around to grab a quick meal, to take in a ball game, or just to knock around. Early on, he struck me as an incredibly busy man, with a lot of responsibilities, but as he got a bit older, and we all got a little more steeped in the study group and in our routines, he still wasn't part of our circle. He lived too far away. He was from an older generation. He held his emotions in check. And yet all of that was just fine, because he made such a strong contribution to the group when we were together every other Monday afternoon.

Ted used to say that Dr. Davies wasn't the type to hang his laundry out on the line, and I suppose that was true. He carried himself like a general. He kept a lot of his views on faith and religion to himself. He addressed the themes of the stories we were reading, but he did so in a circumspect sort of way. His comments were always more theoretical than personal. You could never really tell what he was thinking, and I guess that kept some of the other guys and me at a distance.

Ted was really devastated about this, really grieving, and I'll confess that a lot of the pain and heartache I felt during this period was for him.

Upon reflection, I came to look on Dr. Davies as a giant of a man—but I had known him simply as a man. We'd had a hesitant, arm's-length friendship for all those years, confined to the study group, and that's where it would remain. I thought, *What a shame*. Dr. Davies had had such an interesting, interested mind. He was a fine student of human behavior, and he'd brought a thorough, scholarly approach to our discussions. I couldn't imagine why I'd put off knowing him in all our years together, and now I'd never get the chance. It was a full-on reminder that there's no time like the present to make relationships a priority.

I was concerned for Dr. Davies's adult children. Surely, they were grieving, struggling. In fact, his son had joined us at a few of our sessions over the years, for all I know to keep his father company on the flight, and he even sat in on a session after his father's death. I remember thinking how brave and wonderful it was for a young man to try on his father's routines alongside a group of men he hardly knew, to see if maybe he could find a way forward with a push from his father's closest friend and his partners in study. If maybe God would take an interest and help to set him right.

Dr. Davies had a daughter, too, and I remember reaching out to her in the days and weeks after her parents' death, just as others had reached out to me after my own parents were killed. The connection seemed eerily similar, and I wanted this young woman to know there were people in the world pulling for her and grieving for her. Mostly, I wanted her to know she wasn't alone.

Sure enough, our next session came around on the calendar, and we all made it a point to attend. This alone wasn't unusual, because we *always* made it a point to attend, but there was something else to consider, something new: the death of one of our own, a fellow Bible guy, one of our original members. There was no precedent for such as this, no bylaws or road map for us to follow. We were making it up as we went along, much as we did in those first few sessions back at the University Club, when all we could do was wing it and see what happened. Whatever might happen next for us as a group, we'd figure it out together. All of us.

We were meeting at a restaurant called the Red Robin in those days, over in Easton, and I didn't know what to expect. None of us did. There was none of our usual "pregame" chatter. No talk of our precious Buckeyes. No back-and-forth about our weekends or our kids. We were all conspicuously silent, anxious for our group to convene.

As I sat waiting for the others to arrive, I got to thinking that it was curious how in many ways Dr. Davies had stood apart from the rest of us in the study group. He'd had this special friendship with Ted, and recently he'd enjoyed a burgeoning friendship with Mark Bechtel, who had been particularly excited about forging some sort of professional relationship with Bob. There was also a bond between him and Rondo over the way they had each other's back whenever we discussed the hot-button social issues of the day; they were our resident liberals, so they tended to line up together whenever we talked about issues such as abortion and gay marriage. But other than an annual getaway we'd started organizing a few years earlier, an occasional night on the town, and a holiday gathering we'd taken to having with our families, most of us hadn't really socialized with Bob, which left us processing his sudden death in a kind of vacuum.

Our efforts *off the lodge* in the beginning were fairly transparent attempts at bridging the spaces between our pursuit of meaning and our deepening friendships. We'd come together in this intimate way, joining on an intimate journey, and yet we weren't especially close. Not all of us, anyway, and certainly not at first. We had our separate little constellations of friendships, but we weren't knitted together as a group, except for an hour over lunch every other week. In some ways, it's as if we'd all signed up for the same activity, without really realizing that the relationships we couldn't help but build from all of this intimacy were what would bind us together going forward. Once we realized it, though, we were all over it and looked to help the process along in whatever ways we could. We started arranging great nights on the town, a couple of times a year. We rented a limousine and went from club to club, all over Columbus, listening to local bands, drinking beer, and having a grand old time. It wasn't just about kicking back and making merry, of course. I'm sure we talked heatedly about faith and spirituality and all that good stuff, but after a while, the friendships we hadn't started out seeking were now taking root. Ted wouldn't join us on these nights, unfortunately, because he doesn't drink and doesn't much care to be around people who do. And Dr. Davies never attended these more raucous sessions, mostly because of the distance, but that still left a hearty core of us.

Soon we started taking our act on the road on an annual golf trip. Very quickly, this became a highlight on our calendars, not least because of the memorable study sessions we'd attempt each morning before heading out to the course. These sessions were only variously successful, I'm afraid. Once, I made a wholehearted but apparently half-baked attempt at leading a session myself. I actually thought it went pretty well, but Dick

Vogt sidled up to me afterward and said, "John, that had to be the absolute worst Bible study I've ever attended."

I couldn't argue with him.

Nowadays, we get our families together for a picnic or a holiday gathering of some kind. We talk on the phone more and more. We e-mail. We text. It's become an ongoing conversation, with our sessions over lunch at the Monte now standing as a kind of centerpiece to our time together.

We've become the first responders in one another's lives, but when we lost Bob Davies so swiftly, we weren't quite there yet. We were on our way but not quite there, so in addition to the jarring anguish of loss, there was a deep and sudden regret. On the one hand, we'd lost a dear friend; on the other, we'd lost someone we all wished we'd gotten to know a whole lot better; and when we held those two hands apart . . . well, it's as if we lost a piece of ourselves.

That first session was painful. We talked a lot about *how* something like this could have happened. We talked a lot about *why* something like this could have happened. We looked like crazy for God's hand. We drifted. We struggled. We wondered together what it might mean, if it meant anything at all.

We'd never talked all that much about death before this session at the Red Robin. At least, we were never made to confront our own death, and here, without even thinking about it, we looked to Dick Vogt for a bit of guidance. Back before I ever met him, Dick suffered a pretty serious stroke. He'd had a number of strokes over the years, but this first one nearly killed him, and yet, when he looks back on the experience, he says he doesn't remember being afraid or anxious. Like many of us, Dick had wondered what that transition would be like, moving from this world to the next. It's what we were wondering that afternoon at the study in regard to Dr. Davies. But Dick suggested that Bob Davies, of all people, would surely have met that transition with great courage.

"You'll see," he said to our group with complete conviction. "We'll each have our time, and when our times come, we'll meet it without any fear."

It took a guy like Dick Vogt, a man of disarming candor and abundant good cheer, to articulate what many of us were thinking around that table at just that moment. This was a guy who'd had a vision while walking on a country road. A guy who'd faced his own mortality and come back from that with an even stronger sense of faith and purpose. A guy who wasn't afraid to say what needed to be said.

Years later, a few of us got to talking about Dr. Davies. It wasn't the first time we'd talked about him, of course, and it certainly wouldn't be the last. That's how it often goes. We reach past the years and call back a previous conversation as if it had happened the week before; we keep each other in mind; we remember an observation or an aside that continues to echo within us. And here we got into Dr. Davies's endlessly inquiring mind and the ways it had informed our studies. I couldn't sleep that night after we'd brought all of this up, and as I lay in bed, staring at the ceiling, I started to see a whole mess of similarities between what had happened to Bob and his wife and what had happened to my parents. I'd never made the connection before, other than to recognize the eerie similarities enough to reach out to Dr. Davies's daughter. Both couples had great love affairs, reaching all the way into their twilight years. Both were finally enjoying their time together in a full-on way. And yet their lives were not without struggle or heartache, just as all our lives are not without struggle or heartache. As I tossed and turned that restless night, I came to believe the connection was significant. And most significant of all, both couples died suddenly in a senseless, tragic accident, cheated of the chance to grow old together or see their children onto a more positive, purposeful path.

Looking back, it's a wonder to me that we didn't process our feelings about Dr. Davies's death as a group. We went at it, as part of that first session right after he died, and we kept coming back to it over the years, but we never really talked about what it meant to us *as a group* to lose one of our own like that. We were lost, I guess, and fumbling. To this day, Ted's not sure why he didn't spend any substantive time on it, but I suppose there was no right way to go about it. You just press on. You look for touchstones in the scripture. You go through the motions and hope like crazy that time does its job and helps with the healing.

Rondo remembers feeling the weight of what was unsaid in the Red Robin that afternoon, how it was almost like waiting for some other shoe to drop and then never hearing that second fall.

Mark was probably the most troubled of our group that we didn't deal with Dr. Davies's death more openly or straightforwardly in that first session after his crash. He says, "I like to think that we've learned from that, about how much we mean to one another. And how much we need one another."

I suppose we were all right to feel conflicted about how to proceed, and yet it was understood that we would certainly proceed. It was a given. We hadn't started out as a social group, but the years had bound us together in ways we could never have imagined. I don't think we were ready to deal with that just then. Or we didn't look at the study group in this way, not yet.

Most likely, it took losing one of our own to get us to reconsider what we meant to one another. In that respect, Bob's death was a cruel wake-up call. It was such a monumental loss, and yet we seemed determined to take it in stride. Make no mistake, we were each hurting over Bob's death, in our separate ways. But there's also no denying that we could have used the time to lean on one another instead of leaning on the Book, as we always did. We used the prism of the Bible to help us filter our emotions, at a time when we might have done well to set the Book aside.

We were a band of brothers, and we would be strengthened by this loss despite ourselves. In the years since, the group has become more personal, and I have to think there's a connection. More and more these days, we talk about what's troubling us, at home or at work. If one of our wives is sick, we stand in support. If one of us is experiencing some sort of professional uncertainty, we see how it looks to the group. Not too long ago, we spent a bunch of time talking about the changing shape of Mark's medical practice, all set against the backdrop of the Good Book. We've become closer, more involved in one another's lives, and it's been a happy outgrowth of our intellectual and spiritual pursuits. But at the time of Bob Davies's plane crash, all we could do was turn back to the word of God, to seek meaning and truth and resonance in the stories of the Old and New Testaments, to remember our fallen friend by what we had all built together—what we were building still.

EIGHT

Returning to Speed

THERE WERE TWO OTHER DEFECTIONS OVER THE YEARS, owing to changes in circumstance, so we were back in recruiting mode soon enough. First, Coach McQuaid pulled away with regrets after a good long run. He felt he had no choice. He was a car salesman, and our noon-hour sessions were running into his prime selling time on the showroom floor. When things got a little tough in the automobile industry, he could no longer justify the time away from work.

We all understood—hey, you've got to do what you've got to do. On a strictly selfish and personal level, though, I hated seeing Coach leave the fold, because the study group seemed to have had a profound effect on him. In turn, he'd had a big impact on the group. He brought a practical, no-nonsense perspective to our sessions, which can sometimes get pretty abstract and highfalutin. We had a habit of wading knee-deep into the mess and morass of a particular story and getting tangled in some obscure line of theological mumbo-jumbo, but Coach had a way of pulling us back to reality and helping to root our conversations in real-world terms. I remember being pleasantly surprised at this when he first joined, although I guess I shouldn't have been surprised at all, because he was the same way when we talked down at the gym.

Over time, we came to rely on Coach's character to keep us "real" as a group. It was somewhat ironic, I think, that the weight and worry over practical, real-world concerns would ultimately be what drove a down-to-earth guy like Bob McQuaid from our study, but that only served to remind us that we can't dwell on theory and speculation.

Sometimes life gets in the way, even of our eternal pursuits.

It's been a couple of years, but a lot of the guys still keep in touch with Coach, and I count this as a happy outgrowth of his time with our group. Dick Vogt, in particular, considers Bob one of his closest friends, and from time to time, we'll call him up and tell him we're keeping his seat for him at the Monte.

That's not just a line with us, by the way. We *really* mean it. Once you're in, you're in; once you're one of us, you're one of us. If life pulls you away from the group for a stretch, you'll always be welcomed back. Coach is constantly asking one or another of us if we're still meeting down at the Monte, saying he'll try to drop by, and a part of me half expects to see him each time out.

That's also how I feel about my friend Craig MacDonald, who was transferred to the Pacific Northwest around the same time Coach had to step away. I look up from the table and am stunned that these guys aren't there. Dr. Davies, too. For the longest time, these guys were so much a part of what we were doing that I haven't gotten used to the fact that they're no longer doing it.

Craig had no choice but to make the move, even though he hated what it meant in terms of the study group. He looked at every way he could to keep up with us. We all agreed that it would have been a pretty wicked commute, trekking back to Columbus every other week, although for a time, we tried to make it work for Craig in a long-distance way. We set it up so he could call in. We put one of our cell phones on speaker and left it in the middle of the table, but there was so much background noise at the Monte that we couldn't really hear one another. It turned out to be more of a distraction than anything else. We had to keep repeating ourselves, and it cut into the conversation, so we abandoned the effort before long.

I still talk to Craig all the time. He's become one of my favorite people in the world and one of my closest friends. We started out as golfing buddies and grew into something richer and more meaningful as a result of the study group, which is not to say, of course, that there can't be anything rich or meaningful between golfing buddies.

Ted still sends Craig our talking-point sheets before each session, and Craig continues with his reading. He weighs in from time to time if there's a compelling point he'd like to make. If he's planning a trip back to Ohio to reconnect with friends and family, he'll be sure to do so over one of our Mondays so he can sit in. And he'll often call me on a Monday night just to see how things went that afternoon. The group remains a part of him, even though he can no longer participate in a full-on way.

Not too long ago, when I asked Craig to reflect on his time in the study so I might include his thoughts in this book, he said there was a hole in his heart since leaving our group. I realized I felt the same way about losing Craig. Not just from the group but from my *life*. Yeah, cell phones and e-mail and instant messages are a great way to keep in *contact*, but they're not the same as keeping in *touch*—and here I realized that the study had helped to connect us in such a profound way that the miles between us couldn't quite cover it up.

Here again, life kept getting in the way.

Coach's conflict and Craig's transfer meant that we now had some spots to fill—and I looked first to my old pal Bob Blair. Blair and I went back a long way. He'd known about the study almost from its inception, and Columbus is the kind of town where you tend to know a lot of the same people, so he was friendly with a number of guys in our group. He'd never expressed any interest in joining us over the years, but he knew what we were up to, so I started working on him again. I thought Blair would be a great addition. He'd gotten to know Rondo pretty well, so I had old Red work on him, too. Eventually, our full-court press wore poor Blair down. He agreed to come to the Monte one Monday to check us out.

Blair was skeptical at first. He came with an open mind, he says, but he thought we'd turn out to be fire-and-brimstone holy rollers, speaking in tongues, even though we'd assured him that we were just a bunch of regular guys. In any case, he wasn't the most spiritual guy in the world. He wasn't too keen on organized religion. It wasn't his thing. In particular, he wasn't very fond of the clergy. This was one of his pet peeves, and we used to get into some heated discussions about it. He'd say, "These ministers, they preach and they preach, but they don't talk *to* people. They talk *at* them."

I'd allow that this was sometimes the case, but it wasn't the norm, and it certainly shouldn't put him off to what we were able to accomplish. Still, he wasn't happy that our group was being led by Ted Smith, even though I tried to tell him that the Holy Man wasn't at all like other ministers. He would have much preferred a more communal effort, where we all took turns leading the discussion, but it wasn't a deal breaker for him. Now, of course, Blair holds Ted in very high regard; he can't imagine participating in the study without him.

"I wasn't looking for anything like this when I finally decided to join," Blair says now. "You go through your life, and all you can think about is career, career, career. But then you wake up one day and realize you're gonna be done with your career at some point. Then what will you do? That's where I was in my head, when John and Rondo were trying to convince me, this time around, and they got me to think maybe a thing like this could help me find some of those answers."

Mostly, Blair says he responded to the life-study aspects of our time together. He liked that we could sit down and talk about anything and everything, what was going on with our families, with our work, with our friends and neighbors. As it happened, he came to us at a particularly vulnerable time in his life; he'd just lost his sister, after a long and terrible illness, and he was still reeling, still mourning.

Recently, Blair told me that his first few months in the study group were a great comfort to him, because underneath his grief, he began to see the blessings his sister had managed to collect in her life. He considered himself a "doubting Thomas" at the time; he wasn't even sure if he believed in God or, if he did, what that belief might mean in his daily life. But after hanging out with us a few times, he began to take a different view, an eternal view. Even his sister's illness turned out to be a kind of blessing, he came to believe, because it allowed her to live her life, repair her relationships, and check out on her own terms. This shift in perspective helped him discover his faith at long last.

"It's a choice you can make," he explained to me one afternoon. "There'd be no point to our time on earth unless there was something more for us. What would be the point of a child getting sick at a year or two of age if there wasn't something more?"

Tim Bainbridge rounded out our group about a year later, in the summer of 2008. I'd known Tim for a long time by this point. He'd been active in the Republican Party when I was just starting out in politics, and he'd been helpful to me on a number of occasions. We kept running into each other at different events, and we liked each other well enough. A couple of years after we first met, we started attending the same Episcopal church, St. John's in Worthington. They used to have a Wednesday-night service that lasted about a half-hour, and we kept seeing each other there, too. It's as if we were on each other's schedule.

I couldn't help but notice Tim in church. He was so reverent, so respectful. He wasn't just going through the motions, you could tell, and we'd sometimes stop to chat on our way out. I was always struck by his thoughtfulness, his kindness. We argued over theology at times, but only in a warm-hearted, well-meaning way; instead of locking horns, we'd end our discussions by pleasantly agreeing to disagree. I came away from these discussions thinking he might make a good addition to the study group, so I rolled it over in my mind. I knew we probably needed to add another voice soon, but at the same time, I was careful not to disrupt the fine chemistry we had recently achieved with the addition of Bob Blair. Yes, we'd been built over a long time, and by this point, we were surely road-tested, but it was also a fragile enterprise; the wrong person could send us careening into disarray and disquiet just as surely as the right person could help us sharpen our focus.

I shared my thoughts with Roach, who also knew Tim pretty well. They worked out together, usually in the early morning. They also got along well enough, and Roach agreed that Tim would be a strong addition. We mulled it over for another day or two, and then Roach extended an invitation the next time he saw Tim down at the gym. Tim knew all about our group, of course. Between Roach and me, we'd pretty much talked his ear off about it. So Roach didn't have to do a whole lot of setup or explanation. He just said, "Would you like to join us?"

And Tim said, without hesitation, "Yes, I would."

What I liked about Tim, as soon as he joined the group, was that he didn't write anything down. He comes prepared, make no mistake. But he was like me—in this one regard, at least. Most of the guys scribble their notes all over Ted's study sheets, but Tim just reads the assigned pages, looks at Ted's questions, and formulates his opinions. Once we get going, he speaks his mind. It was clear to me from his very first study session that Tim was hungry to explore and expand his knowledge and his faith. He's so refreshingly honest about the impact faith has on his life at any given time. Now and then, he'll admit to a moment of doubt or uncertainty, or he'll worry that he falls short, but he gets it, he surely does.

In Tim's case, the study has been an affirmation of his faith. With guys like Rondo, Mark, and Blair, it's helped to establish a foundation of faith, but Tim came to us as a fully formed spiritual person. The only piece missing was a place to talk about his faith. He brought this up in the Monte parking lot one afternoon, after he'd been with us for about a year. We'd just finished a spirited discussion of Acts 1, during which Ted had pressed us to consider where we found the Kingdom of God here on earth. It was a central question, but we could only go around and around on it, until finally, Tim suggested that the answer had to do with the study group itself. "Think about it," he said. "We don't talk to our kids about this stuff. We don't talk to our wives. They're great, don't me wrong, we love them dearly, but where do we turn to examine the weight of the world and what's to come? We turn to one another. That's where we find the Kingdom of God. It lives in all of us, of course, but we find it more forcefully when we get together. We find it by our example."

I thought that was a great way to put it, but as soon as he said it, I realized it was insight like this that makes Tim ideally suited to the study group. He gives voice to what the rest of us are thinking, and he hasn't been at it so long that he can't remember if what he means to say has been said already.

"It's been a beacon for me," Tim says of our group, "because if I didn't have you guys, I wouldn't have anyone to talk to about this type of thing. It reminds me that these values aren't just for church. They're not just in the Bible. Here, we're just a bunch of everyday people, putting them into practice. That's a great comfort to me, because sometimes you wonder if that's true out there. I'd never had that before joining the study group. Oh, I'd always had faith, I'd always been spiritual, but now I found myself in this group of men where we all had this great faith in one another, and it was enormously exciting to me."

Faith. It's at the core of every discussion we have in the Bible study group, every story we read, every insight we offer. But what does it really mean? Where does it get us in the end? We talk all the time about men of great faith, men like David and Noah, Moses and Abraham, Paul and the Apostles. It's easy enough to take in their stories and simply sit in wonder—and believe me, we do plenty of that. The Bible is laced with wonder: turning water into wine, walking on water, parting the seas, and on and on. Some of these stories are flat-out exciting. Some are just incredible. But for the most part, we're beyond wondering. We want to know what these stories mean, what it meant in biblical times to live a life of faith, and what it means today.

Lately, what we've come up with is this: when you live a life of faith, it can be a liberating thing. Faith is a freeing principle. We tend to think of these memorable, transformative characters in the Bible as having special powers, as if they were plugged in to God through some mystical fiber-optic network, but we don't really know that. We just know that they were men and women of great faith. And we also know this: faith enables you to hold on loosely without letting go. It's like that .38 Special song: "Just hold on loosely, but don't let go." What that means to me is that with faith in God and faith in the future, we're able to operate on a more open plane.

Faith reminds us that the first innings of this ball game will be played out here on earth, but we'll finish the game in the next life. That doesn't mean we can dog it the first few times we take the field, because we know things will turn out all right in the end. It just means we can go at it with some perspective, knowing that the whole game doesn't play out here and that while we're here, we need to play aggressively.

I don't want to belabor the baseball metaphor, but we can't stop at second base with the way we live our lives. We can't coast. We need to round second and head down to third. Hard. We need to keep running, pushing, striving. Giving it our all. That's what all those characters did in the Good Book. They kept running because of their great faith. They realized God's promise, and in so doing, they realized their destiny and the destiny of their people.

David beating back Goliath. Noah building the ark. Moses parting the waters. Abraham fathering a new nation. Paul going off to prison because of his unbending faith. These guys were all rounding second and running headlong into third, and nothing could stop them. What always struck me about David was the way he was prepared. A lot of people in his circumstance might think, *No problem. God's got my back.* That would have been a measure of faith, I suppose, and underneath that thought would have been the idea that he could bank on God's support to see him through. But you can't lie in bed all day long and think God is going to solve all of your problems for you. You can't be complacent. Life doesn't work that way; He doesn't work that way; you've got to do some of the heavy lifting yourself.

David was a shepherd, and that's not an easy job. Thousands of years ago, it was especially difficult. David's brothers weren't much help. They were content to hang around the house or the village while the hard work fell to David. He was out there taking care of the sheep, which meant there were times when he had to fight off lions and bears. He had to corral all those sheep and move them from one pasture to another and devote himself to this back-breaking, painstaking work. In so doing, he prepared himself for his fight against Goliath.

Nobody knew how prepared he was. In fact, David didn't know it himself, but he had faith. When he showed up, everybody laughed. They underestimated him. And then Saul insisted that David wear his armor, but he couldn't move swiftly or freely beneath the weight of it. David stood his ground and said, "Let me do my thing." And he did. He slew Goliath. He showed no fear. He was ready, because he'd put in the hours. It's like what Malcolm Gladwell writes in his great book *Outliers*. He says everyone who is an expert has to put in ten thousand hours building up his or her expertise. Well, David did just that. He put in his time, and God blessed his work, and it brought about a great change. He went on to become a great warrior. He built the heavenly city. He was not without flaws, of course, but he was a man after God's heart, if you will.

Noah was another man after God's heart. He was out there, building an ark in the middle of the desert, never thinking to question God's will, even if it made no apparent sense. That in itself was pretty astonishing. Everyone was wondering what in the world this guy was doing. It was something they had never seen before. They'd never seen a ship of this size, and they'd certainly never seen someone on such a transparently foolish mission, building it in the heartland nowhere near the water. But Noah was determined. He was rounding second and heading into third, because he believed the survival of the human race depended on it.

Like a lot of people, I'm of two minds on some of these fantastic stories. Some are clearly metaphor and allegory; others stand as a factual recounting of human history, taken from the historical record. I believe it's important to repeat that here, I stand on the side of fact. I believe there was indeed an ark—and not just any ark but an impossibly, unfathomably huge ark—and that Noah undertook this impossibly, unfathomably huge task and completed it heroically. And I don't just *choose* to believe this because it pleases me to do so. I've read a bunch of texts and studied all kinds of histories and have come to the conclusion that there was indeed a man called Noah, who did indeed build a giant ark, which did indeed weather a tremendous flood and, here again, bring about a great change.

The story of Noah has always presented an interesting dilemma for our group. We've read it a couple of times by this point, and each time we have a different take, as a group and to a man. Here's a guy who sets out to do something that's so out there, building a giant ark. You can just imagine how his friends and neighbors might have scratched their heads over his behavior, but that didn't stop him. People must have been stopping by and saying, "You're nuts." Or "What the heck is this guy up to?" But he kept at it. And so we keep coming back to the question of how we would act in our own lives, facing our own impossible tasks. Are you prepared to do certain things that people around you might think crazy simply because you believe in your heart that God wanted you to do them? It's a tough question. And it was certainly tough for Noah, but in his extra efforts, we find something of ourselves.

I can't be certain how I'd act if I was in that kind of spot. I'd like to think I'd have the strength of character and the resolution of faith to answer my calling, but I can't be sure. How do you withstand that kind of scrutiny? How do you measure yourself against the disapproval or disavowal of your entire community? Well, you could come to our little group and test it out. You hold up whatever it is you believe you're meant to do against the weight of scripture. You see how it looks in the eyes of your fellows. You consider how others have responded to the same deal. And you follow your heart.

Now, I happen to believe in Noah, but quite a few of our guys don't. At least, they don't agree on all the details, but the details aren't really the point. Noah's faith, that's the point, his willingness to take a positive action based solely on the fact that he was called to do so. We see examples of this all the time, even among our group. Mark Bechtel faced his own Noah-type dilemma in his professional life when he abandoned his private practice and signed on at the university, where he thought he could do more good. That was a calling, one that meant far more work for a diminished financial reward, but Mark never questioned it. His wife never questioned it. All around him, friends and colleagues let it be known that they thought he was nuts to give up his private practice like that, but Mark was unshakable, because he believed this was what God wanted him to do.

Moses, too, stands for me on the side of history. He was just a normal guy, adopted into royalty, who denounced the life he was living in order to liberate an entire group of people. How a guy like Moses ever returns from his exile to have a private word with the pharaoh is itself remarkable. How do you get that done? It's like calling the Oval Office and asking for an appointment. But Moses was aggressive, and he went at it hard. He was going to get to third base, whatever it took, and when he slid into the bag, he'd managed to free the Israelites from slavery and misery.

Abraham was able to summon enough faith to believe that he could actually father a child. And then, after all those years desperately hoping and praying for a son, he finally had Isaac. But the story didn't end there, as we all know. Abraham took his son to the altar, because in those days, they still practiced human sacrifice, and because he believed that this was what God wanted him to do. He was an obedient and faithful servant. And of course, we know that God ultimately stayed Abraham's hand and that Abraham ended up sacrificing a ram instead.

That's a colossal demonstration of faith. And strength. And a compelling reminder that you can't learn to swim by standing on the shore.

Through Abraham's faith came perspective—on this life and the life to come. His faith that God was good allowed him to exercise tremendous freedom and tremendous personal power. And it wasn't just Abraham; it was all of these men and women, enduring all of these different trials. Their faith helped them to realize there was far more to life than their time on this earth, and that faith and meaning were not about what was going on here.

I'm back to that .38 Special song again: Hold on loosely to this life . . . because we know another life is coming. Hold on loosely to this life . . . but don't let go. Don't take it for granted or waste your talents, but recognize that this is just a way station. Don't phone it in, because this is a time of trial and testing. Don't get caught up in thinking you can merely direct yourself toward the world to come, because it doesn't work like that. It says in the scriptures that it's a sin to bury your talents, and the Bible doesn't want for examples of men and women doing just that.

This kind of absolute faith doesn't end in ancient times, I'm happy to report. There are examples of grace and faith and courage all around, as we live and breathe. I especially admire the example of contemporary women, who stand with certainty in an uncertain world. Aung San Suu Kyi, the young woman from Burma who took such a forceful stand for democracy against a brutal military regime. Anna Politkovskaya, the Russian journalist and human-rights activist who was killed for taking up the cause of the Chechen people and blowing the whistle on her own government. Rosa Parks, who proudly claimed her seat in the front of that bus in Montgomery, Alabama, and jump-started the civil-rights movement. The women in Iran who march bravely through the streets and dare to take off their chadors. These women are everywhere, and all around, and they bring about change on the back of their conviction.

Certainly, some of these strong women found their models in the stories of the Old and New Testaments, but it's clear to me that all of them were answering to a higher power.

NINE

Righteousness

I THOUGHT IT MIGHT BE USEFUL TO OFFER A TRANSCRIPT OF one of our sessions, so that readers could taste the full flavor (and fervor) of the study group. I brought a tape recorder to a session in March 2009 that was fully attended—our first session at capacity in several months, owing to far-flung work and winter schedules. Dick Vogt had been away in Florida for most of the winter; he'd suffered another one of his strokes during that time and had us all worried, even though this one was said to be pretty mild. He seemed to be in fine shape and spirits when he turned up at the Monte on this Monday afternoon.

I'd raced through the assigned passage from Romans 4 earlier that morning. I'll confess, I'm not the best "student" in Ted's class. I'm like our rookie member Tim in my approach. I read the passage, consider Ted's questions, and run it all through in my head; then I get to the session and let it all fly.

My style has been to keep it real, to apply what I'm reading to our modern-day dilemmas, and to put those challenges to the group. Sometimes the weight of the scripture is enough to fill our sessions; other times, we need to work at it and fill in some of the blanks as they apply to whatever is going on in our lives at the time. Most of the guys spend a lot more prep time on this stuff than I do. They make notes. They address the talking points Ted circulates before each meeting. (This week: "How does a person get in good standing with God? How does he 'get it right'?") They write out some questions of their own. Quite a few seek out supplemental readings. I prefer to come at the material in a more spontaneous way, so I tend to just wing it at the meetings. For this session, though, on this particular Monday, I thought I'd do well to revisit the material.

I've always found a lot to like in Romans. It's difficult, because there's a lot going on. I'd forgotten how dense it can be, how consequential. After all, it's where Paul lays out a new agreement between God and man, so it's a pretty thorough distillation of a new covenant. Here on this rereading, I found a lot to like all over again. And a lot to consider. Before Christ, folks did what they could to follow the law. If they broke the law, they made a sacrifice, frequently a fatted calf. In a nutshell, that was it, the default sentence. But Paul's idea was that the law was not the point, because nobody could follow all these laws all the time. No human being could be that righteous, because we're all guilty of envy, lust, and greed.

One sin is just as bad as the other, according to the Bible. There are no small sins and big sins. A sin is a sin, and we visit them all, so Paul put it out there that we shouldn't be excluded from the club, heaven, just because we were human. Our very nature shouldn't do us in.

Paul took the time in Romans to remind us that God is a

perfect being of love. When Christ was among us, Paul writes, He was God incarnate, embodying all the values of God. Truth, virtue, piety, all those good things. So Paul looked at all these laws and all these values and basically said, "Hey, God, gave us a new constitution." Paul explained that God doesn't reject these laws, but he maintained that we humans could never be justified or saved simply by following the law. It's impossible. There was more to it than that, he said. You have to have faith. Faith in God. Faith in Christ. And through that faith, you will overcome your frailties. Through that faith, you will be forgiven your trespasses. You will be justified.

It's pretty interesting and a real departure from how things had been until Christ's time. Paul said that God will declare you righteous through your faith. You no longer have to sacrifice a fatted calf or make a burnt offering because you violated the law. The law is still there, but the law is not the measure, because no one can follow the law. Therefore, we should not be condemned by the law.

Of course, you're still supposed to make the effort. It's not as if the law doesn't matter. It's not as if we can come and go and do as we wish. Without the law, there'd be chaos. Paul comes right out and says that in Romans. But he also calls for a new approach. Faith in Christ. It was a revolutionary thought at the time to suggest that the law is not the point. The effort is the point. The best intentions. The pureness of our hearts. With Romans, we learn that there's no longer any point in sacrificing a fatted calf, say, because Jesus Christ has now made the ultimate sacrifice for all mankind, in such a way that all who believe in Him will themselves enjoy eternal salvation. That's why they call Jesus the Lamb of God in the Bible, because he's the sacrificial lamb.

This is where we raise our game. This is where Christ

promises us a helper who allows us, through prayer and effort, to rise above the muck and mire of this world. But that's hard to do, so that's why He sends us the Holy Spirit, who lives in all of us, and along with that comes a kind of mandate to help us measure how we're doing. It's all laid out for us right there in Romans, and whether you believe or not, it certainly offers a great litmus test for every human being. How are we doing? What can we change? How can we do better?

Ted broke it down for us with a neat little checklist, culled from Romans, chapter 12:

1. *Dedicate your body (energy, time, ability, thought) to clean and active Christian living.*

2. *Have your values, goals, and interests adjusted to the will of God, rather than to what society promotes.*

3. *Exhibit humility, produced by faith.*

4. *Use your abilities in a gracious manner for the good of all.*

5. *Develop a strong distaste within yourself for whatever you know to be wrong, and hold tenaciously to whatever you know to be right and good.*

6. *Care deeply about the welfare, well-being, and promotion of others.*

7. *Serve God.*

8. *Hang in there in unpleasant, difficult times.*

9. *Be generous and friendly.*

10. *Be good to persons who treat you badly.*

11. Identify with other people's circumstances.

12. Be humble, and associate with humble people.

13. Don't retaliate.

14. Be agreeable, not argumentative.

Keep in mind, this is just a checklist. Ted didn't expect us to accomplish each goal. He just meant for us to try. I look at it like my golf game. Some days are better than others. I always remember that no one has a perfect game, so I keep practicing, and I know I'll get better the more I practice. But I also remember that someone else has to look at my swing from time to time, to make sure I've got it right.

In case you're wondering about my own faith in Christ, let me be clear. This didn't come easy for me. There's very little dispute that the historical Jesus actually lived. Even the Muslims call him a good prophet. But in my personal exploration, I studied the facts and the behavior of those around Christ to determine whether I believed Jesus really was the son of God who rose from the dead, and from looking at the evidence, I've concluded that He was. I believe that faith is a choice. There isn't proof but evidence that allows us to decide what we believe. From there, we can strengthen our faith.

All of this takes us to the front room at the Monte Carlo on a cool Monday in March. It was not quite spring, but there was a sense of regeneration among our group. As I said, it was the first time we'd all been together in a good long while. It was the first time many of us had seen Dick Vogt since his stroke. We'd all spoken to him on the phone, some of us pretty regularly, but it was good to see him looking fit and sharp.

My first thought, settling into my seat and double-checking with the guys that nobody minded if I recorded this one session, was that there was no place else I'd rather be at that moment than sitting down to lunch with my Bible guys. Nothing I'd rather be doing than trying to put myself in Paul's head when he was writing about this new covenant, thinking about what he was thinking about at the time, and thinking it all through together with these good people.

The Los Angeles Lakers had clinched the NBA Finals the night before, with a convincing win over the Orlando Magic, who had beaten our Cavs in the semifinals, so there wasn't much to keep us from our assigned topic. If it had been a more exciting game or if it didn't still sting a bit that LeBron James and the Cavs were out of it, we might have dwelled on the game for a beat or two, but it only rated a passing mention in our small talk. There was the usual asking after our families. There were snippets of private, sidebar-type conversations that had been going on between some of us since our last session. Plus, this was our first meeting since I'd announced I was running for governor almost two weeks earlier, so a couple of the guys wanted to know how things were going in the campaign. I'd talked to each of them individually in the days since my official kickoff, and they all knew it was coming, but there were congratulations and well wishes all around.

And then we got into it.

TED: Let's consider the context here. In the first two
     pages, Paul is describing the Jewish people who live
     in Rome. He's talking about how a person might be
     in good standing with God Almighty. How does a
     person get it right? It's the question I put out to you
     this week, and it's what Paul is getting at here. He

uses the word *righteousness* eleven times in this one chapter, so he's really driving home that point. So, how do you get it right? It's an interesting question. We tend to talk more in this group about conduct, how it affects your life and lifestyle. Here we're talking about something else, something very subjective, so how do you translate that?

BOB ROACH: I'll start. It seems that this whole thing comes down to faith and deeds, deeds and faith, and of the two, faith is the more important, but you still have to have deeds. You can't have faith on its own without having deeds, because if you live your faith, then you're gonna be doing good things, you're gonna be doing the kinds of things God would have you do, if you truly do have faith. I don't see how it would be possible for anyone to have faith, real faith, and not practice it.

TED: In the fourth chapter, Bob, it's kinda disturbing to me, but Paul here makes a lot out of it that it's not *primarily* performance. By that he means deeds, of course.

MARK: I think it's about your intentions in your daily living. If what you do is based on your faith and your compassion for your fellow man, that's getting it right. If your actions are based strictly on your own ego, or self-agenda, your self-satisfaction, then it's not getting it right. And it's not about doing what you think you're supposed to do, either. It's not quite that black-and-white, but that's the gist of it.

TED: Seems to me that anybody with common sense might not be particularly religious, but with common sense you're gonna treat people right. You're gonna be fair, 'cause you wanna be treated fair. You're gonna be honest, because you want them to be honest. You're gonna do the right thing.

ROACH: I think that's right. Faith is stronger than that . . .

TED: Then you've got to decide what you mean by faith.

ROACH: It's a belief in Jesus, that He's your savior, which is a lot more than doing good deeds. If you have real faith, and I'm not saying I do have this kind of faith, you wouldn't fear anything. You'd have no fear in your life whatsoever.

TIM: It's right here in the beginning paragraph, where it says that faith is the total submission.

(TED *flashes* TIM *a dubious look.*)

TIM (*continuing*): Don't look at me like that. You wrote this study sheet for us. So, you don't believe what you wrote, then?

TED: Generally, when you use the word *faith*, you're talking about when you walk out the door over there at the front of the restaurant, you have a reasonable amount of confidence that nobody's gonna hit you with their car. You're relatively certain your car's gonna start up, things like that. Faith, though, that's a huge idea.

DICK: Would you say that faith is your assumption that God and Jesus Christ are the same? Today, tomorrow, and always? Do you have faith that they will always be? That's my feeling about it, that this is something you can count on, that there is no difference in God, today and tomorrow. He is always the same.

TED: OK, but why do you believe that?

DICK: Through my faith. Because of my faith.

TED: But why?

DICK: I don't know.

TED: Do you believe in Halloween ghosts?

DICK: No.

TED: The Easter Bunny? Santa Claus?

DICK: No, but I believe in Jesus Christ, and that He's with me today, tomorrow, and always.

TED: But why?

DICK: Because of my experiences in life, I guess.

TED: Ah . . . now we're getting somewhere. In the first two chapters of this book, Romans, it says that people who have not had any exposure to the Bible or to the concept of God or Jesus Christ can still in many instances have a kind of faith. It's within us somehow. It's innate. I've dropped this on you guys about forty-eight times by now, but here it is again. That time I was hiking back in the mountains in the Philippines, and I saw this bowl of food before a tree. Something put there by faith or some divine act. Maybe by a supreme being. There was no explanation for it. And so, to me, that was an act of faith.

ME: So, what are we really talking about here? Aren't we just saying that faith is hope in things not seen?

TED: That sounds unreasonable, doesn't it?

DICK: Well, faith doesn't necessarily mean faith in Jesus Christ.

TED: I think you're right. We're talking about faith in general. Overall faith.

ROACH: So if we didn't have the Book, if we didn't have all this history and all these experiences to draw from, we'd have faith in some other thing out there, probably.

TED: That's right.

ME: You know what, though? If you're a Catholic, I don't know how it is these days, but for many, many decades, maybe longer, the Bible was very deemphasized. I never read the Bible until I was in my forties. Never really read it. I knew some of the stories from when I was a kid, I could quote a couple passages, but I never spent time with it. There are a lot of people like that, right? And yet you can meet some scrub woman who has more faith than anyone you could ever hope to meet, and it's just like falling off a log for her. That's why I think there is an element of faith that's a gift from God. We all know people like that, right? They don't need to study it or understand it. They just take it on faith.

RONDO: That goes back to what you were talking about before, Jack.

(A reminder, just to keep things from getting confusing, Rondo calls me Jack. I can't say for sure how he came up with that. To further confuse, I call him Red.)

RONDO *(continuing)*: They take it on faith because it's not seen. They believe in something, they don't even know where it comes from.

ME: Take it one step further. If faith is hope in things not seen, we don't know that our car's gonna start. We don't know if people are gonna be here at the Monte at noon. We don't know that, we just have faith. In something unseen. But we all knew it was gonna happen. We all knew we'd all be here for the study.

TED: But that was based on experiences that you had. All those other Mondays.

ROACH: Faith is coming here and if there's only three people here, then we know everyone is still all right, and everyone's heart is still in the right place, even though they're not here. So, because there are only three people here, we don't go, "Oh, my goodness, what's going on?" We don't worry that the others might have lost their faith, or that they don't like us anymore, or they don't like Jesus anymore. Faith is being able to accept those things that otherwise will cause you problems. To go through tough times, because you have faith that everything will work out.

TED: Somebody said, "If you have faith, you don't have any fear."

ROACH: Yeah, I think that's right.

TED: But even with faith, there are times when you should be scared, under certain circumstances.

TIM: Sometimes you're afraid or scared initially, until you have time to reflect, and your faith kicks in.

TED: Like trying to figure out what's wrong with your wife, with the doctors and all? You have the faith that everything's gonna work out OK?

DICK: I don't believe that if you have faith, you don't fear anything. I believe you've got to fear God, first and foremost.

ROACH: Well, yeah, that's why you have faith. I fear God. Here we get into that old argument. Are you doing this so you won't be punished, or are you doing this because you love God?

TIM: But how much faith do you have? How much faith do you need? I don't have the kind of faith that would send me down to the creek and walk on water. Is there a limit?

TED: Some years ago now, there was a guy out to show another fella how to do that, and he took four or five steps out across the lake, in the dark. And the other guy thought, *Well, I can do that if he can*, and he stepped out and promptly fell in the lake and about drowned. The first guy said, "I forgot to show you where the big rocks are."

(There's laughter all around, even though we've all heard this joke from Ted before.)

TED *(continuing)*: I know of many cases where faith is referred to in the scripture, and it's described as faith *in* God or faith *in* Jesus Christ. That's helpful to me, as I try to understand this. I can say, "Do you believe me?" And you might say, "Yes, I believe you wouldn't lie to me about this" or whatever. But that's not the same as saying, "Do you have faith *in* me?" See the difference? And generally speaking, the word is used in those two ways throughout the Bible. Usually *belief* and *faith* mean two different things. It's very rare that they're used interchangeably. Do you believe *in* God? It's another level. The focus is not on facts, as John just pointed out, with things seen or not seen. It goes beyond that. It's faith *in* a person or an idea.

ME: So, if you go back and say that faith is hope in things unseen, well, then God is unseen, right? Faith is the hope that what is unseen can also be real. I look at Romans, and it's like a manifesto. It says the old law is gone, we no longer have to sacrifice the fatted calf. It says that Christ is the sacrifice for all time for all those who have faith in God. That's the good news, right? Faith is so important because if you have faith in God and faith in Christ, you have now been part of washing away the sin, because of your faith in Christ. So I think he lays it out here, the reason faith is so important. Basically, if you don't have faith in God or faith in Christ, then that sacrifice doesn't help you. Paul is a very sophisticated writer here about all of this. Some of it is difficult, but I think that's why it matters. Faith is so important because it gets us to recognize the sacrifice of Christ for all time, for all sins, for all mankind.

TED: So, what's the difference, then, between faith and intelligence? Where do we make room for reason and for facts?

ME: Well, your question about how a man gets faith is a very good one. I think there is an element of evidence that's involved in faith. Because, hey, faith comes from God, right? We are saved by grace through faith.

RONDO: OK, but then, how can you equate, using Ted's examples of those experiences we've all had? You know, that you can walk outside and believe generally that you're not gonna get run over, that your car's gonna start? There's evidence for all that. But the fact that Jesus died for us, to save us . . . the only way you can get that faith is through reading the Bible and believing that the people who wrote that Bible had those experiences, saw those things, and knew them to be true.

TIM: That's just one perspective on it, though. You also have your own experiences in life. Have you been able to do certain things in your life through faith in God? Have certain things happened to you in your life because of your faith in God? So, I think that the two have to go together. Me personally, my faith, I've been blessed in so many different ways, so my blessings give me extra reason to have faith, in addition to the historical perspective of the Bible . . .

MARK: Ted, do you think there are different levels of faith and that your faith grows over time?

TED: There's a verse in the Bible that says precisely that, talks about the faith growing. And it describes three different ways that a man gets faith. One is through familiarity with the holy scripture, that's one, and another is through association with people of faith. And the third is through circumstances. All these different things can happen to you, or around you, and this can build your faith as well, so there are all these different ways you can get faith and that your faith can increase. At one point, Paul writes, "I'd just like to spend some time with you guys so your faith will increase." He's talking about association with people of faith, but I've believed for a long time that faith is basically a choice. It's not unreasonable. It's not irrational. But it goes beyond reason. That brings us back to John's "things not seen" again. I think faith is a choice because I can choose to have faith, and it's not that I'm being silly, ridiculous, or unreasonable, and it's not that I'm flying in the face of intelligence. I think there's a sense in which faith goes beyond. I *choose* to believe. I choose, for example, to believe there's a Creator behind the universe. You know, I can't prove that. I do, however, think there's a fair amount of evidence for it. So, yes, there's a dimension of faith that's basically a choice. Does that sound right to you fellas?

(One of the great things about Ted is that he doesn't always wait for an answer to his own questions, but a few of us seem to nod in agreement.)

TED (*continuing*): There's a verse in the Bible that says faith comes by hearing, and hearing by the word of God. Familiarity with the Book and the things it says and the things it reports, there's some evidence there. Hard evidence can help with faith.

ME: So, why is Abraham credited with being such a faithful man, when he went out and shacked up with the servant girl because Sarah didn't have her baby right away?

MARK: I read an interpretation that Sarah was his sister . . .

ME: Yeah, he did that, too . . .

TED: He's shacking up with the servant girl because when he went beyond faith, he had the faith that one day, he was gonna be the father of a great nation, but his wife was in her nineties and pretty well dried up, so he used his own reason. He thought, *Heck, if I'm gonna have a kid, I'm gonna have to do something about it.* He didn't go down the street and give a prostitute fifty bucks. He went with a girl who was regarded as a member of his family, so I'm inclined to defend Abraham on this. I'm not sure I need to, but he believed it was gonna happen, and he thought he had a part in it . . .

ME: OK, but God didn't tell him that the servant girl was gonna have the baby. God told him that Sarah was gonna have the baby. But now, Abraham shacks up with the servant girl 'cause he's starting to wonder, so what does that tell you? Another example: Saul is waiting for the prophet Nathan to show up, but then he doesn't show up on time, so Saul takes his own action, and Nathan shows up and says you'll be dead today 'cause you went on your own. And then what about Moses? Moses taps the rock to bring the water out, and God says he's not gonna get into the Promised Land. So right there, you have three stories about faith. Abraham is the most faithful. Moses doesn't get into the Promised Land. And old Saul falls on his own sword. Kinda interesting, isn't it? The tests of faith vary from person to person, with different outcomes. Is that the sovereignty of God, then, Ted?

TED: Well, where I am on that is that in every instance, they did what they thought was right. Moses beat the rock because that's what he felt he was supposed to do, to strike the rock and maybe get water. Abraham didn't just decide to lie with the servant girl because he wanted sex. He did it because he felt his future and the future of his race were related to having a kid. So, in each instance, they went on their own initiative, doing what they thought they were supposed to do.

ME: And one got punished, and the other didn't. It's sort of like I'm playing in some baseball game, and God tells me I'm gonna win. What was the score of the Yankees game last night, 15–0, right? So, it's 15–0, bottom of the ninth, and there's two outs, and I'm sorta thinking, *OK, let's get some guys in from the stands.* We need some help here. It's just interesting to me, when people took faith into their own hands and didn't wait. Particularly Saul, because he had that big battle, and he had those troops out there in the field, right? And he was told that he'd committed a horrible sin, that he was gonna fall on his sword, so I guess it shows that there are limits to faith, that God deals with you based on the circumstances. I don't know how to look at that. Three pretty interesting examples and three different results. They all pitched in because at some point, they thought, *Hey, it's the bottom of the ninth, and this game is just about over, and I'd better do something.*

TED: So, what do we learn from that?

ME: Heck, I don't know . . .

(We all laugh, because none of us knows what to make of these contradictory messages, not even Ted.)

MARK: That's the kind of faith I sort of aspire to, but my belief in God is so strong, and I'm so confident that He's in total control of my life and that things will be just fine, but I still wake up in the morning and worry about my son and daughter. I wake up some days and worry about my position at Ohio State or making enough money to put my kids through college.

TED: Do you have that kind of faith?

MARK: No, that's the faith I aspire to. The faith where you feel so strongly that God's in control that you don't worry about anything ever. He'll take care of you. He's the Almighty God, and if you have total faith in Him, you should be able to live without fear or concern and know that things will be all right. At the end of the day, He knows what He's doing, and things will be OK.

ME: Isn't that where we fit in? Because if you take the eleven guys who lived with Him and saw Him raising people from the dead, driving out demons, healing people's hands, making 'em walk, and everything else, and then when it got serious, they all ran, and the only people left were the women, except for John . . . Isn't that a case, though, where we have to show up? I remember when we found out that Bob's father was in that automobile accident. Remember, we drove out to Roach's house, and they were, like, "Well, why are you here?" Isn't that where we have to show up and encourage people and maybe not even say anything? Just be there?

TED: Christ said to Peter, in the last week of His life, "Peter, I have prayed that your faith will not fail." Well, were his prayers answered?

ME: Ultimately, yes, they were.

ROACH: At the end of the day, yes.

(The others all nod in agreement.)

TED: He ran, but he came back and became the guy who gave the name to the church in Rome, where if you guys had any consciences at all, you'd send me over there, because that's the only place I want to go.

(Again, we all laugh.)

TED *(continuing)*: I'm getting old. I could use a trip like that.

TIM: I'm afraid I'm too much like Peter.

TED: Which means you're gonna hang in there at the end. You're not going anywhere.

TIM: I hope you're right.

TED: You *hope* I'm right? Crossing your fingers? Putting a few bucks in the lottery? *I hope.* What does *that* mean?

ME: Dick, why do you think the Good Lord keeps bringing you back? They knock you down on the mat, you get back up again. They knock you down again, and you're right back at it.

DICK: I don't think the Good Lord is ready to receive me. He still thinks I have things to do. I'm not sure what they are. I'm kind of searching out for 'em, but I don't believe I'm done with my search yet, otherwise I'd be gone a long time ago.

TIM: I'm not sure He could handle you in heaven.

(We all laugh.)

DICK *(laughing, too)*: Maybe that's the problem . . .

ME: But isn't that the good news, righteousness? Isn't that just Christ being the sacrifice for all time, for all of us who believe in eternal salvation? Isn't that just great news, that if you really believe it, we're headed to an unbelievable place? And when we get there, if it's as great as we think it is, we're gonna say, "Why didn't we get here sooner?" And "Why were we so worried about everything?" Look, when we get to heaven, God's gonna look at us, and He's gonna tell us stuff. We don't know this, of course, but it'll probably be so simple. He'll just say, "Well, you know, here's what you were supposed to do all along." And we'll just say, "You mean it was that easy?"

TED: "Just love me with all your heart." That's all.

ME: Like it's that easy.

DICK: What do you think, can you have righteousness without faith?

ROACH: There was something in your notes, Ted, from Ecclesiastes. Something about being overrighteous. It made me think righteousness can be a dangerous thing, or it can put you on a slippery slope.

RONDO: I saw that, too. In Ecclesiastes, it talks about all these righteous men who have died and all these wicked men who have lived long lives.

TED: Got another story for you. I heard about this guy, seriously struggling to walk and get around. He's

coughing all the time, all bent over, and then somebody asked him what his secret was. He said, "I've
smoked since I was a little tiny kid, and I drink hard,
and I drink a lot." Then he said, "And I've messed
around a lot, too. Any woman I could lay, that's the
way I've lived." The other guy said, "That's incredible. And just how old *are* you?" And the first guy
said, "I'm thirty-nine."

(We all laugh, even though I think we've all heard this one, too.)

TED (*continuing*): There's a verse, first verse of chapter 11
in Hebrews, says that without faith, it is impossible to
please God. I guess maybe I like that verse because it
doesn't say how much faith. It leaves it open.

TIM: Well, how can we keep our faith from being a roller
coaster? We can be up and down with this thing if
we're not careful.

TED: There are a number of places in the Bible where it
talks about faith increasing. Going up. I'm troubled
by this, when it talks about what you're gonna get
from God, because of faith. Maybe it means just a
certain kernel, because it also talks about growing in
faith. How do you do that? I think we have to look
at those passages where it says that faith comes by
hearing. There's one passage in particular I'm thinking about.

*(He looks around for a copy of the Bible, so he can read from it
directly, but no one can produce one right away.)*

TED (*continuing*): You guys have got to be kidding me! No one's got a Book with 'em?

ROACH (*finally pulling a copy of the Bible from his briefcase*): You want me to look something up?

(*At this, Ted seems to wave his hand. He seems to have moved past whatever point he'd wanted to make, so I jump in.*)

ME: I know a lot of people, they take the view that if you keep pummeling folks with all this stuff, it's bound to come out a certain way. If you're in Karachi, you come out a Muslim. If you're in Delhi, you'll become a Hindu. In Rome, you're a Catholic. They just bang you over the head with this stuff, bang, bang, bang, until it's culturally acceptable. And that's a reason to wonder about faith, isn't it: You start to think, *Is it cultural?* But then, if you go deeper, and I agree with this, you have to go back to the basics. You know, how was the earth created? And in every one of those things, every basic question, it's a decision we make, because you get a vote. You either vote red or black. Did the earth just come about on its own? I don't think so, but then I look at all the evidence and study the scientists and everybody else, and I say, "No." Tim here, he might look at the same evidence and say, "Well, what about my life?" You know, Tim comes from Steubenville, he's built a great law practice, he's got a lot of influence, so he's got his own set of experiences. Bang, there's another vote. So, sometimes I think we have to go back to basics, and I think there are times at which our faith is weak, and other times when it's strong, but it requires an assent. You can't just do it blindly, or you'll be in the rock band Blind Faith, but it's not easy. It's a trial.

MARK: I think that's true. Over the years, we've talked a lot about why we find Christianity attractive, and I think it's the idea that with faith, you can have eternal life, in the spiritual realm. One thing I do every day in the hospital is watch people die, and I've been so impressed with individuals toward the end of their lives, individuals with strong faith, and how that transition is such a tranquil one. You look on, and you realize it's actually not people giving comfort to them, it's them giving comfort to their families. You see that, and you get that it's OK to believe. Then you go to another place, where there is no faith, no belief in God. And there's pain and suffering. For them, death is just taking away their misery, but for people of faith, it's a transition to a better world. A world of peace and comfort. And I see it every day.

TED: But you see why the skeptics scoff at that? You're dying of cancer, so you desperately grab onto some idea that you're gonna survive death? You understand why a skeptic would say, "OK, you believe because you can't stand the thought of nothing. That's why you believe." Is that enough of a reason?

MARK: No, these are people who've developed their faith over the years. Not just sudden converts. You can tell the difference. These are people of faith. Real faith.

TED: Well, that's a good place to end it. Just about one
o'clock here. Let's say a prayer and get back to work.

(We bow our heads, and Bob Roach does the honors.)

ROACH: Dear Lord, Jesus Christ, we thank you for this
beautiful, beautiful day, and the time that you've created for us to come together and read your word, and
talk and live your word, and we're grateful for all of
your blessings. Please, as we go out, help us to be
mindful of people we know who are in need of your
touch, and help us to live the life you would have us
live. In the name of Christ, amen . . .

We made our good-byes and paid our checks. (We've set
it up so that we all get separate checks, by the way, so there's
no haggling over who ordered what.) Then we drifted into the
parking lot in groups of two and three, tying up some of the
loose ends of our discussion, wishing one another good things
for the week ahead. I stopped to chat with Dick Vogt for a bit,
to get a better read on his health and tell him again how glad
I was to see him looking so well. He hadn't sounded all that
great the times I'd talked to him over the phone just after his
stroke, but here he seemed fit and sharp and good to go.

When I finally got into my car and pulled out of the parking lot, I realized we hadn't heard from Bob Blair. All through
lunch, he'd been quiet. Typically, he's one of our most vocal
participants. He's been such a strong addition to the group,
because he challenges just about everything Ted tosses our
way. He does the reading beforehand. He spends time on this
stuff—*real* time. And I worried that maybe I was the reason he
was so quiet.

You see, I'd been carping a bit, to Ted and Rondo and a few of the other guys, about how much time we tend to waste with all of our sidebar conversations. More and more, it seemed to me, we'd talk through the news of the day or developments in our careers or our families, and by the time we'd finally sit down to the study, it could be twelve-fifteen or twelve-twenty, and we'd have frittered away all those moments on nothing much at all. I mean, we're all busy guys. We all carve out this little chunk of time in our busy schedules, and I thought we should be taking better care of it. And I'd say as much whenever I had someone's ear away from the group.

It occurred to me that maybe one of the guys I'd confided in had passed my concerns on to Blair and that he might have thought I was calling him out on this. But I wasn't calling anyone out. It wasn't any one guy. It was all of us, myself included. It just started to seem to me that a kind of drift had set in, and we were getting sidetracked from why we were all there in the first place.

Bob might have been new to the study, but I'd known him a long, long time, so as soon as I put two and two together on this, I called his cell phone.

"Hi, Bob," I said when he picked up. "It's me, John. Wondering why you were so quiet today. Everything all right?"

"Everything's fine," he said. "It's just an intimidating passage. I wasn't sure I really understood it."

"I thought maybe you were mad at me or something," I said. "I thought you heard I was bitching and moaning about how much time we waste on all these sidebars, talking about the ball game and everything else but what we're supposed to be talking about."

"Not at all," he said. "It just, faith, you know, it's a big topic.

The kind of faith Paul was talking about in Romans. I wasn't sure I had anything to contribute."

"Well, what about *that*?" I said. "What you just told me, you could have talked about that. How you felt intimidated by it."

He said, "You think?"

I said, "Yeah, I think. That's all a part of it. How we approach this material. How it affects us. How we try to apply it to our lives. If this idea of faith is so difficult and intimidating, we ought to take a look at that, don't you think?"

He said, "Maybe I should have said something, then."

I said, "Maybe you should have."

Then we talked a little bit about the campaign and a few other matters, and I had to smile to myself at the way the group had become such an integrated, integral part of our lives. We'd come together to talk about these big, big issues, eat some lunch, and then slip back into the rest of our lives—like nothing at all, and everything, all at once.

TEN

Dark Nights of the Soul

L IKE MOST PEOPLE OF FAITH, I HAVE MY DOUBTS AND questions. It can feel to me for a stretch as if I'm firm and clear in my beliefs, but then some piece of news or a bold new idea forces me to search for answers. I'm back and forth, bouncing from solid ground to thin ice and then back again. It happens less and less these days, as I grow more and more certain in my faith and continue my study.

The same can be said for almost everyone in the study group. Most people I know are cut the same way. We all have our ups and downs. Even Ted Smith admits to a doubt or two every now and then. As he says, we're only human, so we struggle. Happily, we take turns with our struggling, which means that when one of our group wavers a bit or struggles with an unanswered question, the rest of us can pick him up and set him right.

I sometimes need more of a pick-me-up than my Bible guys can provide, so I counter my own occasional doubts and questions by giving them voice and thinking them through. I talk to my Bible guys and anyone else who might have some insight on the matter. I go off on my own little tangents. And from time to time, the stuff of my days will spill over into these periods of questioning, which in turn are usually followed by an aggressive search for answers.

We all have our moments, and I've assembled this whole collection of people I can call on to talk me through a crisis or a piece of uncertainty, from ministers and theologians to writers and curious thinkers. I've also been doing an enormous amount of reading of religious texts over the past several years—spiritual essays, thoughts on God and Christianity, scholarly tracts, anything I can get my head around.

Wherever possible, I take what I read and layer it onto the issues I face in my own life. In one book I read not too long ago, it was suggested that we could acquire enormous power if we allow ourselves to be put in the path of God. I won't mention the book or the writer, because I don't want to get into any kind of public back-and-forth on my interpretation, but I do want to share my perspective. The author's idea, which was basic, was that by tapping into the power of God through prayer, ritual, fasting, moments of silence, and all the other ways we might connect with a higher power, we set it up so we're plugged in and ready to receive God's word. It's just like plugging in an appliance, according to this author. If there's no power, it won't work, so we need to plug into the power of God.

Again, it's pretty basic stuff, but I read the book and thought, *OK, this makes sense.* This was something I could get behind—it's as if God is the current that courses through all of us, powering and empowering our days. If we switch ourselves on in this way, if we keep plugged in, we'll be all right, and if we turn ourselves off, we'll be in no position to receive God's word. It's hard to argue with that. The author went on to describe all the great things that have happened for all of these people of faith, and it was quite an impressive list. His point was that these kinds of great and sustaining things can happen for all of us, if we keep open to the "power" of the Almighty. I found myself thinking this was an effective metaphor.

But then I started reading another writer who also suggested that the trials we encounter on this earth are designed to test our faith and build character. It wasn't necessarily a contradictory view, just another way to look at God and religion and the template for living that we've been handed in the Old and New Testaments. The idea here was that when you encounter these trials, if you can find a way to accept them and absorb the burdens, it will shape your soul for its eternal destiny. This, too, made a certain amount of sense, so I signed on to this line of thinking as well. In fact, I called some of my Bible guys to see what they thought, and most of us were in general agreement that even when horrible things happen, we can fight our way through to the other side of them, strengthen our souls, and put ourselves in a position of having more authority in the Kingdom of God.

I reached out to Ted to see if he might have a thought or two I might layer onto my own. A lot of times, I'll look to him to offer up a final word and help place a kind of exclamation point on my thinking. But here he put a different spin on things. He said, "You know, John, the goal isn't to go into the next life and be important."

As soon as he said this, I knew he was right. Searching for

authority is an *earthly* perspective. Upon reflection, I believe the writer wanted us to know that trials can shape us for eternity in a positive way, without self-interest.

As an inveterate explorer, I'm wide open to a well-argued position. If you can make a case for eternity, I'm all over it, and yet on this particular back-and-forth, I wanted to be sure I didn't miss something so I started rereading the books, to see if I might transpose Ted's more earthly perspective onto the writers' more Godly plane. This time, what I got back was that God protects those who operate within the Lord's Prayer. That's what came across on this second reading, and I thought, *OK, I can buy that.* People who are really within the Lord's Prayer receive a special protection.

As I read, I started to get comfortable with the discomfiting notion that people of faith can expect to be spared some of life's trials, which, of course, is a narrow, solipsistic view. (And unbiblical.) Still, I drifted toward this line of thinking and started to believe that the more I studied and prayed, the more I might escape some tragedy or other.

But that's not how it works, is it?

Anyway, there I was, content and complacent, when all of a sudden . . . well, I wasn't. I'd been on a kind of spiritual overload, considering all these different views, and then, in the middle of all this reexamination and reflection, I learned that the daughter of a very dear friend of mine had been diagnosed with an advanced form of cancer. It was a horrible piece of news. I ached for my friend and his daughter and their entire family—and when I looked up from my sadness, I saw there were a lot of other people feeling the same way. You see, there's a real small-town element to life in Columbus, so a lot of the guys in the study also knew this family, and we were all upset about it. We talked about it at the Monte. We talked about it privately, in our separate sidebar conversations between sessions.

It was front and center and all around. And then, in the middle of all this *new* upheaval, I got a phone call from a friend of mine who's an Episcopal bishop. I told him what was going on—what I was reading, the heartbreaking news about my friend's daughter—and hoped he could shed some light on all of it for me. I mean, if we stay within the Lord's Prayer, we're supposed to be protected, right? If we plug into the power of the Almighty, then God's supposed to watch over us. I had to wonder how a man of God might explain this terrible illness. I'd been thinking that if you're in good with the Big Guy, you're OK, but it wasn't quite shaking out that way for my friend and his family. My friend was agnostic, but we'd talked about this type of thing all the time. His wife and daughter were amazingly firm in their faith. He, too, was open to anything, in terms of religion and eternity, but he wasn't convinced. He was a man of hope, I guess you could say, as opposed to a man of faith. His daughter went to church. She believed. As a family, they were good, disciplined, purposeful people. They walked all the right roads.

I was losing a lot of sleep over all of this, and try as I might, I couldn't find any comfort or solace. That's when I got this phone call. I didn't stop to think about how unlikely or astonishing it was that this bishop would call me at a time of such uncertainty, but I was thrilled to hear from him. I laid it all out—the sadness about my friend and his daughter, the swirl of doubt that had kicked up within me, and on and on. I said, "If we stay within the Lord's Prayer, we're supposed to be protected, right? That's what these writers are saying." I read him a couple lines from the books that were giving me trouble.

When I was finished, he said, "It's not that simple, John.

Life doesn't work that way. Evil reaches down to people over generations. Faith alone doesn't guarantee protection from the evils and sins of this world. Remember, though, that through it all, God is in charge, and He loves us."

I really love this bishop. He's a great friend of mine, and we have some wonderful conversations. I couldn't help but marvel that he'd thought to call out of the blue like this at such a pivotal time. This alone might have been evidence of God's hand, but for the time being, I was just grateful to have my friend's ear. He's a normal, regular guy. We drink wine together and laugh about all kinds of normal, regular things. But he's also a bishop and a deep man of God, so I gave special weight to his insights. What he was saying really shook me up, the idea that justice or retribution can be completely random, like some sort of spiritual male-pattern baldness, and by the time I got off the phone, the crisis of faith that had been brewing had taken full and frightening shape. Mother Teresa famously called this type of crisis "the dark night of the soul," a term she borrowed from John of the Cross, and that about says it all.

Lord knows, there were a great many dark nights ahead as I tried to figure all this out. I was really struggling. No, this devastating news about my friend's daughter didn't affect me or my family directly, but I ached for my friend and his family. I couldn't understand it or make any kind of sense of it alongside all these other convictions of all these other deep thinkers. It put me in such a low, despairing place. Life and death suddenly seemed so random. It felt to me like a toss-up. *Heads, God wins; tails, I lose.* In other words, when good things happened in my life, I guessed that meant God had blessed me. When bad things happened, I guessed that meant I had no choice but to suck it up and go along with it, hoping that in the end, God might make all things work out to the good for those who loved Him. Or He might not, and I had to be OK with that, too.

It didn't seem like a fair equation, just a random string of possibilities. After all, what is faith all about if having faith means only that God gets all the credit when something good happens and none of the blame when something bad happens? What kind of relationship is that? All the time, you hear people in the ministry say, "You need to love God." Or, "You need to love your trials." It struck me as such a giant rip-off. I was in no mind to love my trials just then. How can you love somebody that allows these bad things to happen? OK, so maybe He doesn't make them happen, but He allows them to happen. It still seemed like a raw deal. And then, somehow, out of all these trials and all this pain and suffering, we're supposed to find strength and look ahead with hope and reverence and all that good stuff. Tell me, what kind of a deal is *that*?

I don't think I slept more than an hour or two that night. Mostly, I stared at the ceiling and the numbers on the digital clock beside my bed. I tried to reach back out to my bishop friend the next day, but I couldn't get through. I tried another minister friend I often talked to about these weighty issues, and I couldn't reach him, either. I guess it was a busy time in the dark-night-of-the-soul department, but I kept pressing for answers. I have a whole collection of these guys, and eventually I got someone on the phone who had some time for me on this. This third minister, Kevin Maney, tried to put these dilemmas in context for me. It was early in the morning, and we really got into it. I was on vacation in Florida with Karen and the kids; I stepped outside onto the patio so I wouldn't wake anyone up.

Kevin said, "I don't know why these bad things happen, John. I truly don't. I can't tell you why we have to go through these trials. But here's what I do know. I know that Jesus came to earth, that He is God, and that He told us how God expects us to live our lives. And once we embrace what He told us were the keys to living, then we should just basically live our lives in faith and trust. That's all you can do."

We went back and forth on this for an hour or so, and at one point, I got so loud and excited on my end that Karen opened the window and whisper-shouted to me to keep quiet. But I was so stirred up, I couldn't keep quiet, so I stepped all the way out into the yard, where no one could hear me.

Kevin's take resonated with me. It took me back to the basics. Do I trust that I have enough faith to believe that no matter what is happening, God is in charge? Even if it makes no sense? Even if I can't understand it at the time?

Kevin's push set me right—for the time being, at least. It was a humbling view, and I was quick to embrace it, but before I signed on fully to it, I reached out to Ted one final time. The Holy Man is the master of the basics. It's one of his themes, that faith and hope and all that good stuff flow from our willingness to accept a few basic truths. I figured that since so much of my faith was in Ted's hands through our Bible study group, I ought to give him the last word, and after I brought him up to speed on what was going on with my friend's daughter and how it came on top of all these other hesitations, he thought about it long and hard. Of course, he knew the broad strokes of that story, because we'd talked about it at length in the study and he'd been in on some of the back-and-forth, in-between discussions as well, but I filled him in on the very latest.

Ted can be extremely careful with his words, as if he's on some kind of budget. After a few long beats, he said, "John, the profound doubts you're having right now are not unusual. Great people have had doubts like this, so let's get back to basics."

I might have seen that one coming. With Ted, when he tells you he's getting back to basics, he means *all the way back to basics.* He even wrote them down for me on a sheet of paper I now keep tacked above my desk at home for ready reference.

Here's what he wrote:

There is firm evidence that the universe had a beginning, therefore it had a cause.

Life in the universe is astoundingly balanced, tuned to an incomprehensible precision for the existence of life.

We do have sufficient evidence regarding God as the foundation for faith. We don't have proof, we have evidence.

If God does not exist, life is futile. If God does exist, then life is meaningful.

Faith is a choice.

Objective moral values have existed since Creation.

Here—no surprise—Ted told me to go back to my very basic beliefs, so that's what I did. (When Ted tells me to do something, I tend to listen.) I knew in my life that God must have worked miracles, because there's no way all the riches I enjoyed came about because of me, from my wife to my kids to my success in politics to the material comforts I'd gained through my work in the private sector. I didn't believe that all these things had happened to me because I was lucky, and I didn't really believe I was good or deserving enough to have made them all happen myself. So I had to think that God had existed in my life all along, in some way or another. Yes, some very bad things have happened, but the good has outweighed the bad, and I don't have to be beaten over the head with a baseball bat for God to get my attention.

Ted could see he was making a dent in my thinking, so he

kept at it. He said, "We look at the definition of trials differently."

I said, "Well, maybe we ought to look at them as experiences that help to shape us. Maybe we ought to leave room for the possibility that some of those experiences might be extremely positive. They don't all have to be negative."

It was a real watershed moment for me, interpreting the biblical concept of trials in just this way and knowing we can be put to the test in success as surely as we can in struggle. Mercifully, it helped me to resuscitate my faith in the wake of all this instability. It took considering all these different points of view and sorting through the mess of my own emotions to remind me where I was with this thing—and, blessedly, that was right where I'd left off. Believing deeply. Knowing wholeheartedly. Trusting in God to see me through whatever trials, good or bad, might come my way.

I set out these particular trials as a reminder that we can be resolute and unshakable in our faith, even though the branches of that faith can sometimes bend in the harsh winds of our days. In some cases, they can bend to the point of breaking, but if you play it right, you can keep them from snapping. I'd been working on this stuff pretty diligently since the day I lost my parents, and I thought I had it pretty much covered. Then these doubts started creeping up on me, harsh winds started howling, and I found myself back at the basic question: Is there a God?

In this one respect, at least, I guess I'm like a lot of people. We all have our low moments. We all get perilously close to snapping those branches. Even a guy like Ted Smith, who's devoted his life to God and the never-ending exploration of faith, asks himself the same question, along with every conceivable follow-up: How does life work? How can we absorb these trials? Can we learn from them? Can we trust that at the other end of each ordeal, God will hold sway?

We can, I finally realized. We must. And so, we press on, knowing full well that we'll bump into another one of these dark nights before too terribly long.

I want to get back to my agnostic friend and his own developing anguish, which, of course, was much more unsettling than my personal crisis of faith, because the way I learned his daughter was sick was surprising. I found out because he called me, which on its face doesn't sound all that surprising, but you have to know this guy to understand what a remarkable leap it was for him to pick up the phone. He was a deeply private person. We'd talked through a lot of weighty personal issues over the years, but there was a line he wouldn't cross when it came to matters involving his family. I certainly respected that line, and yet he called me to tell me this bad news about his daughter. He said, "I'm calling you, John, because I just need someone to talk to."

It was such a stunning turn, and not just because my friend was despairing about his daughter but because he called at all. He did so, I think, because he knew I spent a lot of time on this stuff, and he knew that I cared deeply about him and his family. He reached out in despair, plain and simple. And when someone reaches out to you in a time of desperate need, you reach back. You help them to grab on, in whatever ways you can. Clearly, my friend was shaken to his roots over his daughter's diagnosis, but it wasn't so clear how I could help him or even *if* I could help him. The only thing to do, really, was to be there for him, to be present in his pain, so I kept calling him. I didn't run and hide from his overwhelming grief. Every few days, I checked in with him to see how he was doing. I invited him to lunch or dinner. If he wasn't around, I'd leave a message to let him know I was thinking of him and his family. I didn't want to be a pest, but I didn't want to let things slide.

One night, I did manage to reach my friend on the phone, but he was distracted, distraught. I'd caught him at a tough time. His daughter was due to hear from her doctor the next day, and the expectation was that they'd be in for some more bad news. I couldn't imagine that kind of anguish and uncertainty. It must have been simply unbearable, but he was soldiering on because that's what you do. This wasn't a man who believed in God, even though he was open to the *possibility* of God. This wasn't a man of prayer. This was a man of hope—and so, he hoped. He wasn't up to meeting me for dinner, but he was going about his days and hoping against hope that things would turn out OK.

Still, what he was going through weighed on me, so much so that later that night, I told Karen I had to go out for a drive to clear my head, which was filled with concern and prayers and conflicted thoughts about God's hand. As it happened, we had a prescription waiting to be picked up at our neighborhood drugstore, which was still open at that hour, so I gave myself an errand. It was something to do, and while I was out, I decided to stop for some ice cream. It was a miserable fall night—hail and rain and sleet and every other lousy element known to the season—and yet, for some reason, ice cream seemed like a good idea.

Normally, I'd go to the supermarket for my ice-cream fix, but I found myself wandering into a boutique scoop shop around the corner from the pharmacy, where the cost of ice cream can run pretty high. I'm a well-known cheapskate to my friends and family, so this was unusual for me, but I was being pulled along on this dreary night by a whim . . . and something else.

There was a small cluster of people at the counter when I walked in, and I shared a few pleasantries with them as I made for the door. Before I could head back out into the rain, though, the door swung open, and in walked a pretty young woman with a man and two children. From the looks of things, she appeared to be pregnant with another child as well. I didn't recognize this family at first, but the woman walked straight toward me, her face brightening as she approached.

"Hi, John," she said, extending her hand. "I don't know if you remember me." She introduced herself—and I nearly fell to the floor. It was my friend's daughter, the young woman who'd just received that awful diagnosis and who was expecting even more bad news tomorrow. We'd met before, many times, but I didn't know her well enough to recognize her—not out of context, certainly. She was about the last person I expected to see out on this miserable night. And yet there she was.

I said, "Wow, it's great to see you." And it was.

She must have known I'd been talking to her father, because she spoke as though I already knew about her condition. She was bubbly and cheerful and very positive. She said, "It's so strange running into you here of all places."

"I know," I said. "I never come in here."

"We don't, either," she said. "We haven't even had our dinner, and we felt like some ice cream."

We both smiled at the odd, wonderful coincidence.

Now, as I write this, I wonder if indeed this was a chance encounter. Coincidence? That's hard to say. Providence, hard to deny.

"You look great," I said. And she did.

"Well," she said, "everybody says I'm strong, and I don't

want to be, but I guess somebody's got to be the strong one. Everybody in my church is praying for me, but what I really want is for them to look at my trial and to find their faith. They're praying for me, and the whole time I'm praying for them."

I thought that was a fairly brave and astonishing point of view, given what this young woman was facing. I didn't know it at the time, but her doctors were not treating her cancer as aggressively as they wanted to because of her concern for her unborn child—just another example of her selfless faith. And then, before I could ask how she was feeling or faring, she turned her thoughts and prayers to my friend. She said, "Mostly, I want my father to find his faith through all of this."

You could have knocked me over with a feather. I couldn't believe the strength, and the strength of character, of this young woman, out for some ice cream with her husband and two children on a perfectly miserable winter night, facing a perfectly miserable prognosis with her cancer, thinking not of herself but of others.

I said, "You know, there's a story in the Bible where Jesus looks at a woman and marvels at her faith, and I've got to tell you, if He were in here right now, He'd be marveling at your faith. It's just incredible."

Indeed, it was, and the most incredible piece was that this courageous young woman didn't see her faith as anything extraordinary. It was just a part of her package, a given. She reminded me of Job, actually. Her body was being ravaged by cancer, and all she could do was offer her prayers for her father and for her fellow parishioners. If it were me, I'd be lying in the street somewhere, having people come over every five minutes telling me that everything would be OK. The absolute, resolute faith of this selfless young woman was dazzling to me, almost as if there was joy in it. She seemed to move about with peace and confidence. She was delightful, really. A revelation. And as I share her story here, I wonder how it was that I was placed in its middle—or, more accurately, on its periphery—at a time in my life when the underpinnings of my own faith were so loose and uncertain. I was struggling *because of* what this young woman was being made to endure, and here she was, by her example giving me the strength I needed to withstand that very struggle. It was unbelievable.

I started thinking about all these different points of connection on the drive home. I didn't think this serendipitous encounter with my friend's daughter was just serendipitous, even though I don't believe God works the details of our lives in quite this way. Still, I came away thinking there was something more to it than mere chance. I wondered if maybe it had to do with my relationship with this young woman's father, if maybe the strength of her convictions regarding her faith had something to do with his search for meaning in his life. Or maybe it was tied into the wavering convictions I'd been having over the previous weeks, as I ratcheted up the search for meaning in my own life.

Whatever it meant, however it came about, it left me to wonder yet again how God allows this kind of terrible illness into the lives of such good, caring people. Of course, even not-so-good and not-so-caring people shouldn't have to suffer, and yet there's no end to our suffering. Surely, He allows us to live in a world where sickness and sin are everywhere, and they affect all of us. They do. I'd been thinking that if I bought my membership in the club of Jesus and kept up with my dues and stuck to the bylaws, it would come with some guarantees. At the very least, it'd get me some kind of free pass or the comfort of knowing that my trials were not so bad because they would help me in some way in the next world. And that might have been true, for all I knew, but I didn't know it in my bones in such a deep and fundamental way that I could have persuaded my friend to sign on for the same deal.

My friend and I had talked about this kind of thing before his daughter became sick, but in a sidelong way. We played golf quite often, and every once in a while, I'd make some smart alecky remark about how God was watching over my short game, and he'd say, "Oh, trying to lay the Big Guy on me, huh?" I'd be up by a couple of shots, and he'd think I was trying to rattle him, so he'd be rattling me right back.

But I couldn't go to him now, in these moments of despair, and lay the Big Guy on him, because that could have just set him off on an entirely different path. Plus, it wouldn't have been my place. That was something he had to discover for himself—or not. Maybe his daughter could go to him with something like this, but not me.

What did I do? I went back home and wrote my friend a note. I wrote about how I'd been angry and confused and shaken and how meeting his beautiful, courageous daughter in that ice-cream store had shaken the uncertainty from me. It was such a profound gift, running into her like that and seeing the manifestation of such unbending, unyielding faith. At first, I didn't send the note, because I couldn't decide if it was about me or my friend's daughter, and yet I finally put it in the mail when I realized it wasn't about any one thing. It was about all of us, really. At the time, my thoughts loomed for me as a source of strength and comfort, just as this young woman stood before me as a source of strength and comfort. Whatever she was going through, whatever she was facing, all she seemed to care about was that people should find their faith through her trial, her father most of all.

The fact that our paths aligned in just this way, on a dark and stormy night of the soul, was just short of incredible. And it helped to place me back down on the path I'd been traveling, before all these doubts and uncertainties had crept into my thinking. I'd really been struggling, but this chance encounter set me right and left me realizing that good things will continue to happen, in my life and in the lives of the people close to me, and that very bad things will continue to happen, too. There will be pain, and there will be no shelter, but I choose to believe. I choose to look at the evidence and conclude that there is a God who loves me and that somehow, through the pain, through seeing really bad things happen to others and knowing these same bad things can (and probably will) someday happen to me, I'll figure out how to get through it. And maybe I could even gain from all this pain and suffering, because I certainly gained from my parents' death.

It's a hell of a way to gain, and if it's the only way to gain, then I'm not so sure I want to gain anymore—but it's out of our hands, right?

ELEVEN

Turning the Tables

ONE OF THE GREAT OUTGROWTHS OF THE BIBLE STUDY group and our shared search for meaning is how we've fit ourselves into one another's lives.

Here's a compelling example. I got a call not too long ago from Ted, who seemed to be struggling. He's devoted his life to the word of God, but even Ted has his doubts every once in a while. It's inevitable, unavoidable. It's human nature. He's like the rest of us slobs in the group, working through this stuff, trying to make sense of it all and to live more meaningfully, with the key difference being that he spends all of his time on it. We get to set it aside and focus on our work or on some of the other, more mundane aspects of our lives, but Ted doesn't really have that luxury.

This *is* his work.

"Jack," he said when I picked up the phone. (Lately, he's

taken up Rondo's nickname for me, but he only seems to use it when I'm getting the better of an argument or when he's working his way through some difficulty or other.) "I'm having one of those dark nights of the soul you like to talk about."

Now, that wasn't my phrase, of course. I first came across it in the writings of Mother Teresa, who examined what it meant to people when they can no longer feel God in their lives. They don't deny God, and they don't run away from God, but they can't feel Him the same way they had, and she called this the dark night of the soul. I thought it was a pretty apt description of how we sometimes feel at our lowest moments. Indeed, I'd just told Ted a couple of weeks earlier about that buddy of mine, trying to make sense of his daughter's illness. I'd used the phrase a bunch of times when I shared the story with the study group, and it quickly became a kind of buzz phrase in and around the Monte, as a few of the other guys started sharing their own moments of doubt and crisis.

To hear it back from Ted like this told me he was on shaky ground. I wanted to drop whatever I was doing and try to talk him through it, but he'd caught me at a lousy time. I was heading into a building where I was already late to give a speech, so I promised to return the call the moment I was through.

I got back to him as soon as I could. I said, "What's wrong, Ted?"

He said, "I've got a bad case of the blues."

I said, "What do you mean?"

He couldn't quite put his finger on it. He tried, but he was talking around whatever was gnawing at him. He started telling me this long story about a man he'd been counseling who was having some very serious substance-abuse problems and some other problems with the law. Try as he might, Ted couldn't seem to help him. It was a compelling story, but I didn't see any connection. There was reason for concern, of course. But despair? I just didn't see it. Nevertheless, Ted thought perhaps his inability to turn this guy around might be contributing to the funk he was in.

He said, "I can't say for sure what it is, Jack. But it's frustrating. You want to be able to make a difference for someone."

I agreed with him on that, and yet the more we talked, the more I thought his funk and frustration had to do with something else. He'd let slip a couple comments about his various aches and pains and some other physical difficulties he'd been having, so I thought maybe this was what was troubling him. Ted is not a young man. Anyway, he's not as young as he'd have us think. He looks young. He acts young. His physical appearance and demeanor certainly argue for youth. Plus, he seems to move about effortlessly, gracefully. He was a very good athlete as a younger man—a basketball player, mostly, but he excelled on most fields—and he still carries himself like an athlete. I always admired how he moved about with such confidence, such purpose, such ease. But now I got to thinking how people struggle as they age, particularly as they try to accept that they can no longer do the things they used to be able to do, at least not with the same effortless grace. And then I got to wondering if maybe Ted's physical limitations were starting to catch up with him.

I suppose one of the reasons I was wondering along these lines was that I'd just finished reading in Augustine about how we ought to celebrate our vigor and our relative youth when we can, since the time comes for all of us when that will be gone, and no human being can turn back the clock. Naturally, we don't need Augustine to spell this out for us, but he said it so brilliantly that it really registered with me, and I thought maybe this tied into what Ted was experiencing. Sure enough, the longer we talked, the more convinced I became that this was at the heart of what was troubling him. Nobody likes to get old, right? And here was this tall, graceful athlete not being able to do the things he was used to doing without a conscious thought or a focused effort.

We weren't on the same page just yet, however. Ted still believed his troubles had something to do with his ministry. He worried, for example, that he wasn't making any kind of real impact with our group, that we were only spinning our wheels after all these years. Of course, I immediately tried to dissuade him of this notion. I told him what he meant to all of us, what the study meant to all of us, and Ted seemed really to appreciate that. I don't know that he believed me wholeheartedly, but he did seem to appreciate it.

Then I reminded him of something Rondo had just said to me before our most recent study session. He had a conflict on his schedule that was going to keep him from our table at the Monte, and he called me to talk about it because *I* was the conflict. Rondo had been working diligently and selflessly on my gubernatorial campaign, and he'd bumped into a meeting he needed to attend on my behalf that happened to be taking place on a Monday at noon, one of *our* Mondays. Poor Rondo was torn. He knew I needed him at that political meeting. He knew he needed to be there. It was essential to the campaign. But he also felt he needed to be at the study. He said, "Jack, the study is the most important thing I do in my life. I hate to miss it."

I said, "I hate for you to miss it, too."

This was true. It always felt to me as if we were off our game as a group when we weren't at full strength, hobbled in some way. And I particularly hated that Red couldn't be at the session because of my campaign, but that's just how it goes sometimes.

I told the guys what Rondo had said about not being able to join us, and most of them echoed the sentiment about having to play "short-handed." I thought this was a good time to remind Ted of that exchange.

I said, "You heard what everyone said at the last session. You heard what Rondo said, how he hated to miss one of our meetings. You know how much this means to all of us."

He said, "I suppose I do."

And yet this wasn't it, I could tell. Deep down, he knew he was having an impact. It might have been nice to hear it, but he didn't need to hear it. Besides, it's only natural, as we get a little bit older and look at what we've accomplished, in many cases at what we're accomplishing still, for us to wonder what we're contributing, what kind of footprint we're leaving behind.

But there was something else troubling the Holy Man that day on the phone. For some reason, I thought of my uncle George, who's been a great inspiration to me throughout my life. He's kept young and vibrant all the way into his 80s, and his secret is that he exercises every day. I don't know why, but I drew a line from what Ted was going through to my uncle George and said, "Ted, are you exercising?"

The question seemed to take him by surprise. He said. "Not really."

I suggested he rope his wife into some kind of workout routine. I said, "You and Betty can do it together."

He said, "You know, it's not easy for Betty, either. She's getting a bit older, too."

(I'm treading lightly here, because Betty will likely wring both our necks if she reads this account—Ted's for suggesting that she's getting on in years and mine for repeating his suggestion.)

I said, "But you were such a marvelous athlete. I find it hard to believe a guy like you wouldn't be doing some type of exercise. Just get out and walk a bit. That ought to do it."

He said, "You know, Jack, you're probably right." And as soon as he acquiesced on this, I could feel his mood brightening on the other end of the phone. It's as if he saw a way out of his funk, all on the back of the idea that he could recapture some vim and vigor. A spring in his step, that's all he needed.

We talked for a bit more, about nothing much at all, and when he finally seemed like his good old self, I told Ted I had to sign off. I was racing to another appointment, but I was thrilled that he appeared to be OK. He was thrilled, too. He said, "Thanks for calling, brother." He always calls me that, too. *Brother.* "Good talking to you, bro'," he'll say, and I'll think. *How about that? An eightysomething guy, calling me bro'* . . .

A couple of days later, I called to check in, to see how my young-at-heart friend was faring with his new exercise regime. I said, "How ya doin', Ted?"

He told me he was doing just fine, but then he went off on a whole other tangent that left me thinking maybe he wasn't. He sounded overwhelmed. He went into a long explanation about a series of nine scriptural lessons he was preparing for a study he was going to lead at his old church out in Troy. He went on and on about the mountain of work he was facing.

I interrupted him and asked, "How's the exercise coming?"

My friend the Holy Man, whenever he doesn't have a good answer for something, goes silent. It was as if the phone went dead. For a few long moments, he said nothing. Finally, sheepishly, he said, "Well, John, I know I've got to get about it, but I've been so busy with planning these lessons, I just haven't had time."

Now it was my turn to go silent. I didn't know what to say. Heck, I didn't have a clue. It seemed that on that last call, I'd had Ted's ear and his enthusiasm. I didn't want to be a pest. I didn't think it was my place. And now he had me thinking that if I came down too hard on him over this, I'd lose any shot I might have still had at getting through to him. So I thought about it for another few beats.

And then it came to me.

I said, "Well, that's all well and good, Ted, but you know how you're always checking up on me, wanting to know if I'm doing my fifteen minutes of prayer each day?"

I had told him years earlier that I tried to carve out fifteen minutes at some point each day, and from time to time, he'll keep on me about it, wanting to make sure I'm not slipping.

He said, "Sure."

I said, "Well, I'm so busy with the campaign and all the other stuff I'm doing that I just don't have time to pray."

Once again, Ted went silent on the other end—but then he burst out laughing. Once he caught his breath after laughing so hard, he said, "Why, you dirty dog! You got me!"

This time, he got the message, and as I hung up the phone, I realized that there are times in this life when the student becomes the teacher, and the teacher the student. I took some time to wonder about that and about Ted's role in the lives of us Bible guys. He's been like a father to me. We argue at times. We differ in our approaches to certain things. But ultimately, I look to him for guidance and uplift and an occasional word of reassurance. And he has the same type of relationship with everyone in the study group. He makes time for all of us, and he makes what we're doing a priority, which is why it's become such a priority for us, why a guy like Rondo has to miss a session with a heavy heart, even when he's got something else he needs to do.

Yes, every now and then, the teacher and the student can

switch things up on each other, but at the same time, we must remember that no man is above his master. We can help each other out and lift each other up, but it's important scriptually to keep those roles distinct. No student is ever above his teacher; no servant is ever above his master.

At the end of the day, Ted is the teacher. My Bible guys and I are the students. And it all shakes out to the good.

TWELVE

Grace and Truth and Fast Food

THINGS DON'T ALWAYS GO ACCORDING TO PLAN WITH ME and my Bible guys. I don't mean that a discussion gets away from us in one of our sessions or that we never get to any of Ted's talking points or prompts, because that happens with some frequency, I'm afraid. No, the real surprise is that occasionally there are some real surprises, such as the time not too long ago when we arrived at the Monte to find that a gas main had burst and the place was closed.

The temporary closing of the Monte shouldn't have been a big deal, but it was. We only had an hour. A group of guys grooved into routine can't shift on the fly and switch things up without a little stress and strain. Mostly, though, it was a big deal because we'd all been looking forward to this session for the previous two weeks, and for a couple of moments, it appeared we'd have to scrap it. We were all really disappointed. That's how it goes, I guess, which is why we're still at it; as soon as one session wraps, we look ahead to the next one, and it looms on our calendars as a refreshing point of pause in our workaday lives, a chance to recharge our eternal batteries, replenish our souls, analyze our recent behavior, and steel ourselves for the week ahead. We keep reaching out to one another between sessions. We call. We e-mail. Some of us even get together, sometimes with our wives and our families. We keep the conversation going, but it's always aimed at the next study session. That's where it all comes together for us, and that's why we all look forward to it, and now here we were in that strip-mall parking lot, in the middle of our busy day, trying to figure out if there was a place where we could get a bite to eat and somehow salvage the week's study session.

It set us off on a curious adventure, that's for sure.

Predictably, there were no other lunch places in that particular mall, which meant we'd all have to get into our cars and go in search of a new venue. Or we'd carpool and double back to retrieve our cars after lunch. The trouble was, there wasn't a suitable restaurant in the abutting strip malls, either, to the best of anyone's recollection. We racked our heads for a location but kept coming up empty. Try as we might, no one could think of a decent place for us to meet. For a beat or two, in desperation, we talked about running the session right there in the parking lot, like a spiritual tailgating party, and worrying about lunch later, on our own time.

(This would have been a memorable disaster—and with our cars parked nose to nose and our doors flung wide, it's likely a local police cruiser would have pulled into the otherwise empty lot to get to the bottom of our suspicious activity. Imagine the headlines: "Local Pol, Community Leaders Caught in Drive-By Bible Study!")

A few of our guys had yet to arrive, so it fell to us early birds to come up with some kind of substitute plan, but we weren't doing such a good job of it. Finally, Rondo mentioned a Wendy's around the corner on Schrock Road, and you'd never imagine a group of grown men (most of us on some kind of restricted diet) could get so excited about the prospect of a fast-food meal, but in truth, we didn't really care about the food. Rondo assured us that there was a big seating area at this Wendy's where we could put a couple of tables together and have at it. This last was our chief concern.

Anyway, we had no other choice. It was Wendy's or bust, and bust was out of the question.

What an odd scene. There was our group—six or seven of us on that Monday, as I recall—commandeering a cluster of small square tables in the middle of the restaurant, while all around us the weekday lunch regulars were probably scratching their heads. There was a table full of moms with their toddlers in tow. There was another pairing of construction workers, scarfing back some two-fisted square-burger concoction and a set of too-large sodas. There were a couple of salespeople off in the far corner—pharmaceutical reps, I was betting, judging from the big black sample briefcases they'd stuffed under their table. And to complete the picture, a variety of singletons were enduring a lonely lunch that on this day would be laced with some weighty eavesdropping opportunities. They had no choice but to listen in: it was us or those fussy toddlers.

At the Monte, and at our other haunts over the years, we didn't run into too many solo diners, but here at Wendy's, they were everywhere, and they were about to get an earful. We didn't care. In fact, I don't think any of us gave this aspect of our makeshift circumstance a conscious thought, and it's only now as I set this scene to paper that I recognize the absurdity of it. The sheer out-of-placeness. I mean, some of these hungry, busy people had probably thought about hitting the drive-thru lane before deciding to come inside and stretch their legs and enjoy a quick, quiet lunch. They'd come inside for any number of reasons; maybe they had some reading to do or some e-mails to return on their handhelds, and here they suddenly found themselves seated alongside a half-dozen men talking loudly and forcefully about the Bible.

These good people had never seen the likes of us in a place like this, and certainly, none of them had any reason to expect to have to listen to a vigorous discussion of God and man and everything in between.

On the menu for our study that day: envy and justice. A bit of an odd combo, and yet, in many circumstances, they might rest on opposite sides of the same moral coin. Before we could get to these themes, though, we had to wait in that little corral line to get our food, so we took some time settling in. Plus, there were still a couple of stragglers we were attempting to reroute by cell phone to our new location. In all, we lost about a half-hour of our allotted time, and when we'd finally collected our meals and sat down at our slapped-together table, our group was deep into small talk and chit-chat and whatnot. These days, it takes us longer to get started on the actual *study* part of the study group, but on this day, it took us longer still. And yet, somehow, we landed on Ted's assigned topics without really realizing it or meaning to. That's what happens when you're grooved into routine, when you're jumping back into an ongoing conversation. We knew where we were headed, so we started veering off in that direction. We started laughing about the times when one or another of us had been transparently envious or petty or jealous. We were human, after all, so we stepped good-naturedly onto the patch of common ground Ted had scoped out for us this afternoon, ripping into each other as we ripped into the wrappers on our burgers.

The dynamic in our group is much the same as you might find in any other group of American men who've been getting together on a regular basis for a number of years. It doesn't matter if we're studying the Bible or meeting for a regular round of golf, there's a familiarity that develops that casts us as closest friends and harshest critics. We know one another too well by this point for any one of us to let another slide on a lapse or a failing or a faux pas—and it seemed it was my turn to be called on my behavior. A couple of the guys pointed out that I used to complain about my role at Fox News, where I hosted a Saturday night program called *Heartland with John Kasich*.

Bob Blair said, "That was always such a big thing with you, John. Did you win the ratings? Were you number one?"

"You're right," I said, knowing I was beat. "It just killed me to lose to someone else. But that's not really envy. That's more like whining. The fact of the matter is, I've never once woken up in the morning and found myself wishing I was one of those other guys on the air or wishing I had what they had. That's never been the case."

"That's just semantics, John," Bob Roach weighed in, back with his own tray of food and pressing the point. "Whining is just a symptom of envy."

"That could be," I agreed, as our other sidebar conversations seemed to quiet and the group as a whole began to focus on this one line of chatter. "But I'm not in any way, shape, or form trying to put myself up there as perfect."

"None of us is perfect," Tim Bainbridge offered, finally

moving me off the firing line and pushing our discussion along more general lines.

"The last time we discussed envy, we were reading the story of Joseph," Ted reminded us. He explained how Joseph's brothers were probably envious of Joseph's magical coat and how Joseph might have brought some of that on himself by flaunting what he had—and we were off and running.

Soon, our talk of Joseph and his brothers morphed back into our discussion about the ratings I used to get at Fox and then into the ways we measure our success in our own lines of work. One of us asked Roach how it feels when he notices a certain competitor in financial services landing a string of big clients. It must have struck me as a pretty interesting line of thought, because I jumped to pursue it. I said, "How do you deal with that?"

"I think about the things he does better than me," Roach said with great humility. "I think about how I can do things differently."

"Do you ever wonder if he's happier than you?" Mark Bechtel asked. Mark had been one of our stragglers that day, and he'd missed most of our small talk, but he fit himself right in on arrival. He said. "And here I'm not just putting the question to Bob but to the group. When someone has more success than you, when he accomplishes more than you, do you take that to mean that he's also happier?"

Ted said, "My experience has been that riches don't necessarily bring happiness."

I said, "You're probably right on that. So, what would you rather be? Unhappy and poor or unhappy and rich?"

Ted said, "I don't think it matters. If you're unhappy, you're unhappy."

"But why does God allow so much unhappiness?" Blair wondered. "Where's the justice in that?"

"Wouldn't that depend on the basis of the unhappiness?" I asked.

Ted said, "That's what trips a lot of people up. They think if God is just, He would step in. If God is just, a twenty-six-year-old mother of two shouldn't get cancer. If God is just, a drunk driver shouldn't hit my son head-on and put him in the hospital."

"If God is just," Mark added, "how could He let the Holocaust happen?"

"That's probably the worst," Ted said, "but God's justice doesn't mean He intervenes and prevents bad things from happening, just as He cannot set it up so good things keep happening. When we start to think that way, that's when we get off track."

"And it just takes us to the same argument we always have," Blair said. "If God had His hand in everything, if He always intervened, then man wouldn't have free will."

We were on familiar territory here, even in this unfamiliar setting, and as the study unfolded along its usual lines, I found myself pulling back from it—marveling at it, really. Here we were, in a crowded Wendy's restaurant in Columbus, Ohio, on a Monday afternoon, talking about God and envy and justice and all these other substantial issues, while all around us was the heat and haste and hustle of a typical suburban lunch rush. It was such a surreal scene, and yet it was also exactly right, as far as our group was concerned, because we're just a bunch of guys having lunch and kicking things around. It made sense to do so alongside all these other regular folks, going through the motions of their own days, doing whatever they felt they needed to do to get by.

It was all of a piece.

In the end, it was just another study for us, and yet for the first time in twenty years, I realized that what we had built and nurtured in our time together was bigger than any one of us. It was bigger than any set time or place. It was bigger than any tangible or knowable thing. The study had become a part of us in such a way that we could take it with us, even to a crowded fast-food restaurant.

It was who we were, after all.

Now, here's where we broke even further from routine, because after our abbreviated, rerouted session that afternoon, we were still hungry for talk of God. A few of us had to get back to work, but as it happened, another few of us had an open afternoon. I was one of the ones who had to get back to work—specifically, I had to give a speech in Irontown, about a two-hour drive from the Monte parking lot where some of us had left our cars. But there was all that trapped time to fill in the back-and-forth, so I suggested we take our session on the road. I offered it as a tossed-off notion, because I'd be stuck in the car either way, with one of my aides doing the driving. There was no reason to think any of these guys would take me up on the invitation, but three of them did. Ted and our two newest "recruits," Tim Bainbridge and Bob Blair, were inexplicably willing to come along for the ride, and I was grateful for the company.

The miles flew by. We shot right past a small digression on whether or not our family pets can expect to enjoy an afterlife at our sides (it was generally agreed that they could not, by the way) and on to a tangent regarding Karl Marx.

"His big thing was that religion was bogus," Blair offered, referring to Marx. "It was the opiate of the masses."

"That's right," I piped in from the front seat, where I was halfheartedly making some notes for my speech. Politics was second nature to me, while this meaning-of-life stuff was still fresh and invigorating, so I was paying better attention to the latter. Plus, I didn't want to miss any of the chatter in the back seats of our minivan. I said, "Karl Marx was going to separate the bourgeois from the proletariat. He put it out that God was phony, and he worked against religion, and out of that came Stalin, and anybody in the Soviet Union who practiced religion was subject to arrest and imprisonment."

The guys in the study know not to get me started on this type of thing, because once I get going, there can be no stopping me—not a good situation when you're trapped in a car with me and looking at another couple of hours of driving.

"Why do you think that was allowed to happen?" Tim asked. "Why would people in charge be so fearful of organized religion?"

"It's because people of faith hold principles that cannot be destroyed by human beings," I suggested. "That's the Magna Carta, right? The Magna Carta was created to say, 'Look, there's no human being superior to any other human being.' I'm paraphrasing, but that's pretty much the nut of it right there. The only superior being was God, and the Magna Carta established once and for all the superiority of the Creator over the ability of a human being to be a tyrant, so that's why you get into this whole business of mind control. That's why they go after religion and people of faith, because they don't want to deal with the strength that individuals can get from their belief in a higher power."

Blair wondered if that type of thinking was behind our apparent attempt to separate matters of church and state, which pushed a whole new set of buttons on the religion and history fronts. For the longest time, this has been one of my pet peeves, because I've always thought it was one of the goofiest misinterpretations of our founding fathers' intentions. Our founders didn't come out and say that government should be somehow separate from religion, as many people now believe, or that religion was in any way unconstitutional or un-American. In fact, up until the late nineteenth century, there were state-sponsored churches in this country, so clearly that wasn't the case at all. Even Thomas Jefferson, who was viewed as a deist, believed that freedom of religion was essential to our progress as a nation. George Washington said repeatedly and quite movingly that Providence had a hand in everything that had ever happened in his life, good and bad. Divine intervention was everywhere apparent for him. So, clearly, religion held a kind of sway, but the men who drafted the Constitution were in no way frightened or put off by religion. They weren't frightened or put off by the word or the power of God. They were just careful to ensure that our government should not force people to believe a certain way or put any kind of stamp on their faith, so it's funny to me how the impulse behind it has been co-opted over the years—that is, it'd be funny if it wasn't also so distressing.

The values that run through the Old Testament are essentially the same values this country was founded on: honesty, humility, faith, personal responsibility, accountability, being a good friend and neighbor, trusting in our fellow man, and so on. It's the Judeo-Christian ethic, in full force, although quite a few of our guys think the New Testament offers a better, richer, more compassionate template for living.

Bob Blair, for one, considers the Old Testament a little too down and dirty for his tastes. "It would be so much nicer if there was some more softness to it," he said, now that we'd stumbled onto the comparison. "When you think of those stories, they're all blood and guts and murder and mayhem."

"Where are you going with this, Blair?" I said. "There's more evil in what came later. Heck, six million Jews were killed in the Holocaust."

"Yes, but there were fewer people back then," Blair pointed out. "The numbers are relative."

"That's six million, and who knows how many more in China, under Mao Tse Tung," I said, amending my argument.

"But that doesn't change the fact that the Old Testament was pretty brutal," Blair repeated.

"No, I guess it doesn't," I allowed, turning to Ted for clarification. "But that's an old covenant, right? That all changed with the arrival of Christ. Jews still practice the Mosaic covenant, I think. Isn't that right, Ted? They're still back on that Old Testament model."

Ted nodded. "I hope so," he said. "It's a great covenant."

"Right," I agreed, "and Jesus said, 'I did not come to destroy the old law but to fulfill it.' And now there's a new law, grace and truth. Those became the themes of the New Testament. That kind and gentle enough for you, Blair?"

"Grace and truth," Bob repeated, mulling it over. "I like that. I can see that."

"See if this carries any weight," Ted started in. Here again, I could tell from Ted's thoughtful, careful tone that he'd been waiting for a break in our conversation to interject these next few thoughts after doing some mulling of his own and that when no break was forthcoming, he started in anyway. He said, "I'm thinking here of two well-known atheists. Sigmund Freud, the father of psychiatry, certainly one of the most highly regarded thinkers of the past century. There was some controversy there, but he was certainly a great and respected mind. And Karl Marx. There was some controversy there, too. Both were huge influences in their time, in their own way, and both were very aggressive atheists. As intellectuals, they thought they were above God and religion and that sort of thing. There was no place for it in their thinking, and yet both of them died in great despair. Does that have any meaning for you fellas?"

"Meaning what?" Blair asked.

"Meaning does it tell us anything, other than it helps if you're dying to think there's something more ahead?" he said.

"That's a pretty cynical view, don't you think?" Tim said.

"Maybe, maybe not," Ted said, "but it's certainly something that two of the most interesting minds in recent history, these two giants, each of them a card-carrying, flag-waving atheist, came to the ends of their lives in great depression and despair, because they finally realized that what they'd been preaching all along, that your conscious life ends when you die, was just an intolerable, unacceptable thought. The idea that, hey, this is all there is to it was too much for these guys to bear, and when they came face-to-face with this, well, it was unbearable."

"It could be coincidental," Tim suggested. "We don't know the nature of their depression. It's just conjecture that it had to do with a sudden awakening at death's door."

"They were in great pain," Ted repeated. "That's not conjecture. That's been well documented by those who were with them at the end. By their own writings, even."

"But Christians die in great pain," Tim countered. "In physical pain, certainly."

Blair said, "So, basically, what you're saying, Ted, is that if these guys had chosen to believe in an afterlife, in eternity, in God, whatever, they would have been spared all that pain? How can we know that in this case? If there's as much evidence that there's an afterlife as there is that there isn't, how can the simple act of believing, of faith, erase the kind of pain we're talking about here?"

"It's just a theory," Ted said. "Something to think about."

"They could have chosen to believe in an afterlife and still been depressed," I said. "The issue is what constitutes life, *real* life."

"We're just guessing on this one," Tim offered.

This was certainly true enough, but then, there's a lot of guesswork and conjecture in what we do. We imagine what things were like for the people who lived in ancient times, so it makes sense that we imagine the same for our contemporaries.

Lately, we've been discussing how God's relationship with man has evolved over the centuries, in much the same way as a father might change his approach to his son as he matures. Ted's a big proponent of this type of evolution and suggests that man has moved from being treated by God like an infant and then an adolescent and finally a young adult going off to college. Now, he says, God's hand seems to be guiding us the way Ted himself might seek to influence his forty-five-year-old son.

"It's a process," Ted remarked from the back of the van, "and no one can say where we'll be in the next century or the one after that, but I like to think we'll be more autonomous. God will give us a little more rope, a little more responsibility, as long as we demonstrate that we can handle it."

"But we can't handle it," Blair said. "There's so much hatred and greed and violence in this world, what makes you think we can handle it?"

Tim thought to wonder how we've gotten to a place of such discord and disagreement among the world's religious leaders. "Think of it," he said. "Of all the millions and millions of people on this earth, of all the hundreds of religions, the Jews and the Christians are the only ones who worship our God. Yet the numbers don't lie. There are many more people out there who believe wholeheartedly in *their* God, and it boggles my mind how God let this happen. Buddhism, Hinduism . . . they all believe in their own supreme being."

"That's exactly right," Ted said. "And it's been that way since the beginning. Every bit of archeological evidence that exists, every civilization on record, has a sense of a higher power, a greater being, the chief of all chiefs."

"The Buddhists and the Hindus all believe their supreme being is the chief of chiefs," Tim pointed out. "And yet they teach kindness and beauty, the same values that we teach. There's not a whole lot that separates us, when you break it down."

"That's also right," Ted agreed. "Most of the world's religions believe in basic moral values. There's some divergence, of course, but most of them promote honesty, forgiveness, humility, fidelity. They're usually a given."

At this point, we were pulling into the high school where I was meant to give my speech, and as we spilled out of the van, I thought once again how fortunate I was to have friends like these as fellow travelers—not just on this road trip, of course, but on our shared journey. And as I took to the podium that night and started sounding the themes of my speech, I could see my Bible guys lined up along the back wall of the cafeteria—my own private Amen Corner—and I felt a little bit like Lou Gehrig. You know, as if I was the luckiest man on the face of the earth, because I had somehow cobbled together this collection of like-minded friends who could think of no better way to spend their afternoon than to join me on a long drive to the heart of Ohio, just so we could talk about God and religion and the stuff that really matters in our lives.

I thought, *Kasich, it doesn't get any better than this.*

THIRTEEN

Points of Connection

W E DRAW A LINE FROM WHAT WE READ TO HOW WE LIVE. This has been the essence of our time together in the Bible study group, finding ways to attach these ancient texts to our own experiences. It's how we roll—and here we are, more than twenty years later, rolling right along.

Along the way, we've grown our games. We've grown our faith. We've taken the seeds of a lifetime on the sidelines of religion and watched them flourish at one another's side. We've made God and our shared search for meaning a priority in our lives.

This is a great, good thing, I've come to realize. Indeed, we've all realized it in our own ways, but it took sitting down to write this book and pumping my Bible guys with questions about what the study has meant to them for me to get some perspective on it, for me to get *their* perspectives on it. We don't

usually talk about the group itself or what we've come to mean
to one another; we just have at it. But once I started getting
everybody's take, I was thrilled to hear almost all of the guys
say that throwing in on this effort is one of the best decisions
they ever made. Almost all of them say it's helped them to syn-
thesize the ideas they've been carrying around with them since
childhood and to put them into practice. Almost all of them
say they look to our sessions as a highlight of their calendars,
a centerpiece of their lives, and that as a group, we've come to
stand as one another's touchstone. Without really realizing it,
we've become one another's closest friends and surest sounding
boards. We have our separate groups of friends, to be sure; we
have our wives and our families; but there's no supplanting this.

Now, after twenty years, whenever we come to a dilemma
or a crossroads or a crisis point, we wonder what our Bible guys
would do or think or say about a certain situation. We've taken
the resonant and resolutely Christian message of one of the
most prevalent bumper stickers of our generation—"What
would Jesus do?"—and given ourselves another option.

And yet, for all the growth that's come our way as a result
of our time in the study, for all the deepening and sustaining
friendships, we're still celebrating the same values and principles most of us learned as kids. In this one respect, there's
nothing new in what we're doing here. That's the simple beauty
of it, really. There are no groundbreaking discoveries—just the
hard, diligent work of a group of men looking to live more pur-
posefully, more meaningfully.

When you put a new shine to a thing, you can take it in as
if for the first time. It can become luminous and shine brighter
than you ever imagined, and I like to think that's what's happened for me here. I've gone from thinking about this stuff in
theory to living it and breathing it and reaching for it. I try to

put it into practice, and I try to improve myself and the people around me on the back of it. But at the end of each day, at the end of each study session, I'm still the same person I was as a child. I'm still little Johnny Kasich, "Pope," the son of a mail carrier in the small town of McKees Rocks, Pennsylvania. I've still got the same values that were instilled in me by my parents. And in many ways, the world I look out on is the same world that gave me shape. I still keep the same picture in my head of what God looks like, the one I've carried since I was an altar boy at Mother of Sorrows. It's a picture I carry with me every other Monday, when I leave for our study sessions. I see Him with a white beard, sitting on a throne. I see Him smiling, beneficently, approvingly. It's an image I probably borrowed from some illustrated Bible I read as a kid, and it's stayed with me. I can close my eyes and imagine that He is watching over me and that He is good and just and understanding.

The other guys in the group have their own ideas on this, and from time to time, we compare notes. God appears before each of us in His own way. On an intellectual level, I know it doesn't much matter what God looks like or if the picture I hold in my head matches up with anyone else's. And yet I'm curious. It helps to know how others imagine Him. It helps to know I'm not alone.

It helps, too, to know how others pray. Anyway, it's interesting, and we talk about this, too. We run the gamut in our group. We've got guys who hit their knees each night before turning in and guys who pray silently throughout the day. There's no right way to pray, of course, only what feels comfortable.

Lately, I've come to think that God exists outside time, beyond time. There are a number of theologians who've examined this, and it makes a lot of sense. It makes sense to a few of my Bible guys, too. A God who exists outside time can care about every human being all at once, right? A God who exists outside time can dwell in the past, present, and future, because there is no past, present, and future. He can be present at all times. It's a fascinating way to look at eternity and spirituality, and yet I'm not sophisticated enough to fully understand, say, the space-time continuum. I understand that when you travel in a rocket ship, time slows down. I understand this whole speed-of-light business, but after that, you start to lose me. Still, if we can get close to a concept like that and understand it in a scientific, verifiable way, then we can also make room in our thinking for a God who exists outside time. We can begin to open our minds to these other dimensions—and that can be an exciting, liberating way to understand the concept of the Almighty.

One of the big, ongoing discussions we have in the study is the tug and pull we all feel, living in two worlds. There's the here and now, and then there's the hereafter. There's the present, and there's the lessons and legacy of the past. Either way, we're grounded at one end or the other.

Bottom line: I believe we have been placed on this earth for a reason. I believe this in a macro way and in a micro way—in other words, that this is true for all of mankind and also for every man and woman as individuals. We all have talents. Saint Paul talks about how we are all blessed with our individual gifts and how if we put them together, we can create a symphony. I listen for that symphony every day. Some days, it's out there in full force, and other days, I have to strain to pick out the faintest sounds—but there is always music.

Listen carefully, and you can hear it, too.

My experience and the experiences of those around me tell me that God is good. I've seen it in other people's lives. I've seen it in my own life. God is good and just, and at the end of the day, He'll square things up. I know this as surely as I know myself. A skeptic might ask if this is something I know in my bones and in my soul or something I merely choose to believe. Is it some sort of hopeful ideal? Or is there evidence to support it?

Here again, this is the kind of stuff we talk about over lunch at the Monte. This is the music we make, putting our heads and our hearts together in the here and now and looking ahead to the hereafter, trying to give our time on this earth an eternal spin.

We talk about pretty much everything, my Bible guys and me. Over the years, we've probably touched on every human emotion, every human condition, every human frailty, and I thought we'd do well to consider a few of them here.

Forgiveness. One of our greatest hits, I guess you could say. And it's not just us wrestling with such as this. We're all working on repairing our relationships and showing mercy and finding ways to understand the hurtful behavior that invariably finds us. But how do you really forgive somebody who's deliberately tried to hurt you? It's a central question, for our group especially. Every single one of us has been in a position where somebody really tried to hurt us—professionally, personally, across the board.

My buddy Rondo came up with a unique way to deal with this. One day, we were repeating the Lord's Prayer, and I noticed he'd dropped a key line: "Forgive us our trespasses, as we forgive those who trespass against us."

I said, "You forget something, Red?"

And he said, "No, Jack. I dropped that out of the prayer. I don't say it anymore."

We all just laughed. We'd never heard of such a thing. It

reminded me of Jefferson, writing his own Bible. Here Rondo was rewriting the Lord's Prayer. He just took it on himself. The reason, he said, was that in his heart, he simply could not forgive this person who was dragging him through an expensive and long-running lawsuit over some property he was trying to develop. The case just went on and on. Rondo was embittered by the trouble he was put through; it took a big bite out of him. In the end, he prevailed on every single contested point, but there were so many twists and turns to the thing that it proved to be a great strain. It ended up costing him thousands and thousands of dollars. There wasn't a day that went by that Rondo didn't talk to me about it. He talked to all of us. It was a real front-and-center worry.

So, nobody really thought anything of it when he dropped that line from the prayer. It was just Rondo letting off a little steam, but it put me in mind of a line from Augustine, who wrote that whenever you're really angry at somebody, the thing to do is put yourself in that person's shoes and realize that you could very easily be in those shoes yourself. I also thought that if God Himself can forgive mankind for what happened to Christ, then we ought to be able to find a way to forgive our enemies. We crucify Jesus every day by the things we do, and yet He finds a way to forgive us.

So that was that. I figured Red would never utter those words again. He can be pretty stubborn when he sets his mind a certain way, and he appeared set on this—that is, until recently, when he called me on the phone one evening and said, "Jack, I'm starting to think of putting that line back in there." We were in the middle of a conversation about the stock market, our families, my campaign, our busy schedules, and Rondo just dropped this little bombshell, that he was thinking of scrapping his own personal Lord's Prayer.

He said, "It's really been bothering me. Maybe I've got to work on this some more and figure out how to forgive this guy."

Now, for Rondo to make such an about-face was remarkable. It made a powerful impression on us, because we all knew how much he'd been hurt by this lawsuit. We all felt for him on this, because we'd all been hurt or wronged in some way or another, at some time or another. None of us had been inclined to go out and rewrite the Lord's Prayer to suit, but we all appreciated Rondo's stand. So it was great to see him come around on this.

Time has a way of healing things. But you really have to make an effort to get your mind and your heart in the right place. And it takes more than just time. It takes hard work and reflection. It takes a measure of compassion. And Rondo had finally put in that hard work and reflection and was ready to make a kind of peace with what had happened.

Now, whenever he recites the Lord's Prayer, he gives the unedited version, while I listen in and think, *Isn't that something?*

Vanity. Not too long ago, we found ourselves deep into a conversation on self-importance, and one of us pointed out that on a recent trip to his church, the pastor had flashed a sign on the wall that offered two commandments. The first: "Love God." The second: "Love your neighbor as you want your neighbor to love you."

That got us talking, of course, because most of us believed that vanity was just the opposite of that. It's *Love yourself as much as you want your neighbor to love you.* If we're honest, we're all guilty of not always making that extra effort with other people. But I'm working on it. *We're* working on it. Together, we've come to the conclusion that you're prone to this type of thinking whenever you have success in one area. It comes with the territory. When you think about it, humility and vanity are two sides of the same coin. It's a gift, though, when you can get the coin to land on the right side every time.

Integrity. One of my mother's big lines when I was a kid was that no one can ever take your integrity away from you. She was right about that, as she was about most everything else. When I got a bit older, I realized that sometimes integrity comes at a high price. I think about integrity every time I go to a funeral, which happens more and more these days. It comes up without fail. It's what matters after you're gone. I've started to think of it as a savings account. The more integrity you have, the richer you are. But it's better than money, because you can take it with you. If you've lived your life with integrity, that's what people will remember about you. It becomes your legacy, what you leave behind for your children, but it's also something you can take into the next life.

Our talk of integrity put me in mind of an earlier discussion we'd had in our group about David, who at last had an opportunity to kill King Saul after Saul had failed in repeated attempts to kill David. But did David take that opportunity? No, he didn't. A lesser man would have done away with him, but David believed it was wrong to kill an anointed king, for any reason. He had an intimate and proper relationship with God, and knew at bottom that God was God, and he wasn't.

Generosity. I went to church one Sunday, and the minister announced that he was going to let one of the parishioners speak.

I rolled my eyes and thought, *Come on, man. I came here to listen to you, the learned man of the Bible, not some lady sitting next to me.* I was really put off by this, but then the parishioner got up and did an amazing job. She knocked it right out of the park. She said, "Just remember, in the old days, the people who were the best givers gave the fatted calf, not the skinny calf." I remember that sermon as if I heard it yesterday, and in all the years that I've been going to church, I don't think I've ever heard a more direct message than that. That'll teach me to jump to conclusions about people.

Think about this woman's message as it applies to you. Are you giving the fatted calf or the skinny calf? It's one of the hardest things to get right, and yet the concept is spelled out for us in the Bible, where Jesus praises the widow who put almost nothing in the basket for charity. He holds her out as an example and points unfavorably to the wealthy man who gave far more. Indeed, the widow gave what she couldn't afford to give, while the wealthy man could have certainly given more. On a percentage basis, as a reflection of what she had, she gave an enormous amount. The guy with a ton of money gave hardly at all. I get that. I think we all get that. And yet, like most people, I hide behind the notion that a calf is a calf. How much you give is not reflected just in your tax return but in how much you do, how much you give of yourself.

My wife and I are charitable people, but I try to pass off that skinny calf from time to time. I shouldn't, but I do. My fellow Bible guys admit to the same. A lot of us tend to rationalize how much we're giving against what our friends are giving, but it's a deeply personal matter. There's no set equation or formula, just a number or a threshold that feels right.

Here's the deal: if you give, and you tell other people that you gave, then you'll get all the credit you deserve. But who do you want to acknowledge your gift, God or some plaque on the wall? The bottom line is that we need to be happy with what we're giving. We need to feel good about it. It's not to be measured by anyone else but by how we feel inside. We make our own personal deal with the Lord on this one. Nobody else needs to know about it. But we'll know. Absolutely, we'll know.

Ambition. Another one of our recurring themes. It seems to run through a great many stories in the Old and New Testaments, just as it runs through our days. Whenever we land on it, we ask ourselves a basic question: How do you keep one leg in the spiritual world and at the same time keep a leg on this earthly plane? We struggle to find that balance. We're expected to use our talents, whatever those happen to be.

Getting ahead and being successful are important. But it's about keeping a leg in both worlds, the earthly and the eternal. It can be a tricky business. If you don't maintain the right balance, you can fall over. Here's a good example. I was sitting with a politician who was considering whether or not to run for president. I don't want to mention his name here, because it was a private conversation, but I believe I can touch on a few salient points without giving away this guy's identity. I said, "Well, you know, it's gonna take a lot of money to run for president."

He said, "But it's not about money, John. It feels to me like I'm being directed on this, from God above. Like it's my calling."

I said, "Well, you can ask God to sit on your finance committee, but you're the one who's gonna have to make the phone calls."

You've got to realize that you have a responsibility to carry out your personal mission, whatever that mission happens to be. God has given you your talents to succeed, and you have an obligation to do so. If you bury your talents in the ground, it's a sin. But when you do have success, you've also got to realize that a lot of that is attributed to something beyond you. Yeah, you've done all the hard work, but without all the gifts that were placed in your hands, you wouldn't have been able to get it done. The more successful you are, the more you have to reflect on the fact that it's not about you. That's hard to do. Human nature tells us to celebrate ourselves, perhaps even to sing our own praises, but on our best days, we ought to remember that our power, our strength, our gifts all come from above.

There's a story about this in the New Testament. One person buried his talents in service to God; another quietly honed his talents and used them in a small way; the third exploited his talents to the fullest. The message, once again: round second and go headlong into third. And how were these three people judged? The first was severely chastised for not using his talents in service of the community. The second was rewarded in only a meager way, while it was the third person who reaped the biggest reward.

The first time we considered this story, we wondered at the balance we all seek in our lives, but then, we realized that success is not about bringing glory upon ourselves. If you're blessed with a God-given talent, you are meant to use it and to use it fully—because, after all, we perform for the glory of God. We must strive to do good works, to pursue our God-given gifts and abilities to the fullest, and to share the benefits of those good works with others. Remember: "Keep first the kingdom of heaven." It follows that the more we seek the kingdom of heaven, the better off we should be here on this earth. Of course, this is tough to do, but it's an important goal. And it's important to remember that we are the stewards of God's gifts. If we seek success to bring glory to God, ambition is good and wholesome and righteous. It's when we look to bring glory on ourselves that we get into trouble.

Justice. Another tough one. And another biggie. There's a wonderful adage in the Bible: "Don't judge another person when he has a speck in his eye, because you have a log in your own." I read a line like that and set it alongside the stuff of my life and come to the conclusion that judgment is not our job. It's God's job to sort that stuff out.

And let's not forget that justice doesn't always happen here on earth. When we think in our own minds that somebody is getting away with something he shouldn't or that a certain punishment wasn't severe enough to fit the crime, we get frustrated. Sometimes we see justice on this side of the grave, but I have the faith to believe that the ultimate judge, the highest judge, will bring justice in the long run.

I was talking about this with one of my friends and said, "You know, the great thing about God is that if you live here on earth and you don't have a lot of income or a lot of status or an impressive title, the amazing thing is that when you go before the Lord, everyone is judged equally. Your money, your power, your position . . . they don't mean squat. God will look at you and assess your life based on what you did, not on who you were or what you had."

That goes beyond ultimate justice. It's ultimately fair, too, and we talk about that a lot in the study group. Sure, it's hard to accept sometimes.

But that's justice—sometimes now but many times later.

✦ ✦ ✦

Envy. I've always been struck by a line I found in a Scottish prayer book: "Allow me to accept the fact that I've been called to a small task, when my neighbor has been called to a large one." What that means to me is that it's easy to sit back and covet the good fortune of others. Let's face it, it often happens that a competitor or a colleague enjoys a measure of success you believe was meant for you, but how you absorb these inevitable disappointments reveals a great deal about your character, your relationship with God, and your ability to dwell comfortably, happily, and mercifully in your own circumstance.

Once again, tough but worth the effort.

Greed. Consider this line from one of our readings: "Where your heart is, that's where you'll find your treasure." It's amazing how money and the pursuit of money can rot us to the core, and yet, in one way or another, we are all in pursuit. We know better, and at the same time, we don't. Yes, money can offer tremendous security, and it can provide wonderful opportunities, but it can also cloud our thinking. My young daughters have helped me to place the getting-and-spending of my post-political life into context. They memorized a psalm in Sunday school that said, "Store up for ourselves treasures in heaven, where moths and rust do not destroy and thieves do not break in and steal." I hear those words and recognize that there is no security in material things.

Every time I tackle a Bible passage, it's as if for the first time. I read the Bible as a kid, of course, but it didn't speak to me back then. Maybe I wasn't ready for it. Or maybe I didn't know how to take what I was reading and place it alongside my life. They were just stories. Some of them were difficult to understand. But now these stories mean more to me than any other. There's a reason people call them the greatest stories ever told, because they're shot through with every conceivable life lesson—and a few inconceivable ones, as well.

From time to time, I'll pull back from whatever is going on at a study session and consider the picture we make from an outside perspective. At these times, I'm only half listening. What I'm mostly doing is marveling at the scene, thinking, *This is what religion ought to be about.* It's not some syrupy, abstract, elusive thing. It's this right here. It's life. It's making the effort to live more meaningfully. It's building a network of mutual support and fellowship.

It's finding God in the pages of the Good Book and in the stuff of our days.

We're not so full of ourselves in the study to think we have all the answers. In fact, it's just the opposite. We know we fall short of the goals we set for ourselves, but we strive to do our best. We push each other to do better. We make mistakes, but we hope to learn from them. We consider them. We consider, too, how we might make the world a better place. We work on ourselves, but then we open it up. We worry about the decline in our moral values and the disappearing guideposts in a society that seems to be moving away from organized religion. We look at the rootlessness that appears to be taking hold across the country in too many of our communities. We discuss what we might do to set things right, in our own little corner of the world.

One of the reasons we've survived and thrived as a group is that we've made the word of God more accessible. We don't treat the Bible like a set of rules and restrictions. As important, we don't place Ted on any kind of pulpit or vest him with any authority that he doesn't earn each time out by the strength of his insights and arguments. He just sits around the table like the rest of us—with a little more experience, perhaps, but with the same vested interest. Heck, we earn the same authority for ourselves every time we make a compelling point. (And we trade on it every time we take up a boneheaded line of thought.) We're all in this thing together, and the carryover from that is that we're all equal. No one opinion is any more valid than another.

Of course, it follows that our dogged pursuit of richness and meaning is no more compelling than that of any other group of men or women or any other individual. It's just ours, that's all, and I shine a light on it in these pages so that others might look upon it as a kind of beacon and that it might open up a path to richness and meaning in their own lives as well.

That window of opportunity Stu Boehmig talked about just after my parents' death? For me, it opened up onto this right here, and I hope in some small way I've encouraged some of you to peer through the open windows in your own lives. If you're not prepared to crawl through them in a full-on way, then maybe you'll be content to sit beside them for a while. Let's face it, we're all working to improve our lives and to make a little bit of a difference in the lives of others. My Bible guys and I help one another out on this, and in this way, the group has become a kind of shared focal point. It's allowed us to measure our direction by turning to the stories of the Old and New Testaments time and time again. It's allowed us to stand as one another's compass—and together we find our way.

"It's easy to claim that we live in a world of darkness," I wrote in one of my previous books, *Stand for Something: The Battle for America's Soul.* "But there's a lot of lightness out there. And we seem to want to walk in that light, as much as possible."

I believe this is true for my Bible guys and me, as it is for all of us.

"We all have our gifts," I also wrote, "and it falls to us to unwrap them and share them with the rest of the world, and once we do, there will be goodness all around. We find those gifts in this realm by standing up and being counted. Trust in something bigger than yourself, and we shall all be rewarded. Look up into the night sky and know that as the stars shine bright, so, too, shall you. Become a part of the constellation. Have faith."

FOURTEEN

A Closing Thought

MARK BECHTEL AND HIS WIFE, ANNE, CAME OVER FOR A visit on the Friday following Thanksgiving 2009, and their mere presence in our home and in our lives was a testimony to the strength and reach of our group, because over the years, they've become very close friends. Karen and I really look forward to their visits. My girls do, too. The Bechtels are wonderful people, and our relationship has taken on a deep, fine texture since Mark threw in with us Bible guys.

We'd been friends before, which was one of the reasons I asked Mark to join the study but we've grown much closer over the years. At this point, we've watched their kids grow up, just as Mark and Anne are now watching Reese and Emma grow up. Together, we take heart and pride in the accomplishments of all of our children. Right now, Anne and Karen are talking about wedding plans for the Bechtels' daughter, Amy, who was just a little girl back when we all first met. Their son, Jeff, is also making his way in the world and doing well, so there was much to celebrate all around.

One of the great things about the holiday season is the chance it gives us to reconnect with friends and family, as everyone seems to catch their breath and the moving sidewalks of our lives are put on pause. Thanksgiving weekend is usually the kickoff for us, and I've come to relish that time of year—Thanksgiving, Christmas, New Year's—when everything slows down a couple of notches, and we lower the volume and soak everything in.

OK, so that's the setting. There we were, in the holiday moment, in the spirit of the season, enjoying one another's company. I should mention here that Emma and Reese are just crazy about Mark. He always makes a point of carving out some special time for them when he comes to visit. He's great with kids, so he visited with the girls for a while, and as the evening grew long, Karen and I put the kids to bed, and we adults decided to go downstairs to watch a movie in our basement family room.

Before we started the movie, we reflected on our blessings. I said, "You know, these moments of peace are just wonderful, and we really need to take the time to appreciate them and the many riches we have in this world."

Everyone seemed to share the sentiment. There was warmth and great cheer. It was Thanksgiving, so we gave thanks. And then, just as the movie was starting, Anne's cell phone started to vibrate, so she left the room to take the call. This wasn't unusual. As parents, we're always getting called away from whatever we're doing by our children (even our adult, soon-to-be-married children), and it's never really a big deal, so nobody thought anything of it. A couple of minutes later, though, Anne came back into the room looking distraught. Beyond distraught, actually. Shaken and shaking. The call was to tell her that moments earlier, probably just as we were lifting our glasses in a toast, her brother-in-law had slipped and fallen from a silo back home on his farm in Indiana. He was killed instantly.

What a tremendous shock, not just to Anne but to Mark as well. To all of us. We were all stunned into silence. What do you do when you get a piece of news like that? What can you say? Without a coherent word, without a conscious thought, we found ourselves moving up the stairs from the basement, toward the deck that opened out from our living room. It was as if we were being pulled outside into the chill fall air, and once outside, we just started hugging.

At some point, Anne looked at me despairingly and said, "Please, just pray for my sister."

Now I look back on this moment, in the middle of processing this horrible piece of news, this intense grief, and I marvel that Anne's first reaction was to ask us to pray for her sister. It was striking. She could have said or done a thousand different things, but she turned to God. She believed that God could help her sister. She didn't rail and scream, "How could this have happened?" She didn't lash out. She simply implored us to pray for her sister, as she was now doing, of course. So, that's what we did, right there on the porch. We prayed for her sister.

I'd never even met Anne's sister or the brother-in-law who'd just been taken from her, and yet I believed that ultimate faith and prayer was what this family could cling to. What a shocking, devastating, horrible piece of news—and yet what choice did this poor family have but to slog through it? To go through these painful motions until they reached the next point of pause? And what choice did we have, on the sidelines of their grief, but to reach out to them in whatever ways we could? There's a ritual to grief, I've come to realize, so we all set about it, each in our own way, appropriate to our relationship. I kept calling, over the next few days, trying to get through to Anne and Mark to see how they were doing. When I finally reached Anne on the other end of the phone, she reported that her sister and her family seemed to be holding up. "Everybody's in mourning," she said, "but they're gonna make it."

That's about as sad as it gets, and as shocking as it gets, but that's how it goes with bad news. It's always sad, always shocking, but what gets me is that the flip side to bad news is not always so immediate. The bad stuff can hit you straightaway, but the good stuff can sneak back up on you. One moment, you're reeling and overcome with emotion, and the next . . . well, not so much. That's how it shook out for my "agnostic" friend and his pregnant daughter, the one who'd been given that awful prognosis just a few months earlier, the piece of news that had sent me into my most recent spiral. Now, by Thanksgiving, the daughter's cancer appeared to be in remission. Her scans were finally clear. Her baby had been born and was doing great. Everybody was acknowledging that there was still a long road ahead, but hey, it's a long road for all of us.

What a beautiful, hopeful outcome to such a harrowing, sorrowful turn.

The takeaway? Well, it's like Dickens. We live in the best of times and the worst of times, all at once. We drink the good with the bad. All we can do, as it says in the scripture, is build our house on a firm foundation. That's what it comes down to for me. It's important to have faith, not just in bad times but in good times as well. We need to build our house on a rock, not on sand, because we all know the storms will come, and we'll need to weather those storms in our own painstaking way. And the only way to know this and to weather this is to accept that at the end of the day, God is in charge.

My guys and I have still got some work to do. We understand that. Our houses are still under construction. We understand that, too. In fact, we relish it. But we're getting there, and together, we've accepted that our Creator will prevail in the end. He always wins, doesn't He? And somehow, through our sorrows and our joys, we'll endure whatever we're meant to endure—just as I did when my parents were killed, just as my friend's pregnant daughter shouldered her terrible cancer scare, just as Mark Bechtel's in-laws are clinging to faith and hope and one another in their time of grief.

Somehow we'll survive—not only survive but thrive. Build a house on a foundation of stone, and together we will withstand the currents of life, as children of God.

Acknowledgments

A book such as this doesn't just happen.

I am indebted to my cowriter Dan Paisner for his indispensable contributions to this project. His constant probing, pushing, understanding, and compassion for the material were essential. Most important, Dan and I traveled this road together, and our friendship has deepened as a result—and the great additional benefit is that my family has come to love him as well.

I am also grateful to my friends Jai Chabria, Rondo Hartman, the Rev. Dr. Kevin Maney, and Craig MacDonald, who took the time to read the early versions of the manuscript and offer insightful, informed suggestions. Brooke Bodney and Sarah Dove also read over our shoulders as we worked and offered some much-needed encouragement.

Of course, there wouldn't be a book at all without my literary agents, Jenny Bent and John Silbersack, our biggest cheerleaders. I value their friendship, their guidance, their instincts.

It was Jenny who was out in front on this, pushing me to write a book about my faith—an idea I resisted at first, because I just didn't think anybody would care to read about something so profoundly personal.

Peter Borland at Atria/Simon & Schuster believed in this book from the outset, and has been enormously helpful shepherding us toward publication, as has the rest of his "team"—including Judith Curr, Kathleen Schmidt, Lisa Sciambra, Al Madocs, and Nick Simonds.

To my wife, Karen, and my daughters, Reese and Emma, thank you for "keeping it real" for me at home. You are my beacon, and my constant joy.

And finally, to my fellow Bible guys, thank you for putting up with me all these years, and for allowing me to share the story of our study. They were like me at first, wondering who the heck would care about our little group, but by now they've come around and joined me in the hope that what we've been doing in our corner of the world might inspire others on their own version of the same journey.